Praise for *Flowing from the Cross*

Dr. Paavola is upbeat, not ending on the troubles of sin but lifting us to the practical benefits of constant focus on God's forgiveness through Jesus. *Flowing from the Cross* presents foundational truths through an abundance of common, daily images to which we can all easily relate. Arranged conveniently for small-group use, this Christ-centered book can also be helpful to pastors looking for memorable ways to illustrate the many facets of forgiveness in their sermons and classes.

Rev. Dr. Dale A. Meyer, president emeritus, Concordia Seminary, St. Louis

As a communicator, I'm always looking for new ways to convey the unchanging truths of the faith. Dr. Paavola lives in this space of transforming normal, ordinary objects and experiences into eloquent gateways that invite us further into God's kingdom, making the foundational truth of forgiveness an exciting adventure to discover anew and explore with delight. In *Flowing from the Cross*, Paavola engages the senses of sight, touch, and sound as ways to embody the forgiveness offered to us in Christ on the cross. And along the way, I learned new stain-removal tips and the need to buy bigger speakers! As always, thank you, Dr. Paavola.

Amy Bird, MAR, writer for Lutheran Life

God has blessed Dan Paavola with a winsome and captivating communication style, which is abundantly displayed in *Flowing from the Cross*. The center of the Christian faith is the forgiveness of our sins, and Paavola's work provides an extra heartbeat of joy to readers about this truth. [The book is] rich with personal anecdotes, life analogies, hymns, and Scripture; I found myself eager to turn the page so that I could discover new insights, joys, and poignant moments of reflection on God's promises. Paavola's real-life object lessons will surely become sticky and embedded in the reader's mind for years to come.

Dr. Jim Pingel, dean of the School of Education,
Concordia University Wisconsin and Concordia University Ann Arbor

Every sinner should read this book! [It speaks of] forgiveness for you, comfort for you, and it's not generic; it's specific and understandable. This forgiveness is from God through Christ, and it's for you and those around you. [Paavola] knows his audience. He knows the struggles and guilt around us and inside us. He also knows the richness of Scripture, and best of all, he has a marvelous way of illustrating the heart of the Gospel and life-giving love of God. He gets you, he gets the guilt-laden world, and he gives the treasures of Jesus in a way everyone can understand. I gained new insights and applications that I will preach and teach. Every person who reads *Flowing from the Cross* will receive help and lasting hope as we deal with the turmoil surrounding us and inside us. The Gospel refreshes and restores, and so does this book.

Rev. Dr. Allan Buss, president, Northern Illinois District of the LCMS

Receiving and sharing forgiveness stands at the heart of the Christian journey. Dr. Paavola, in his warm and charismatic style, unfolds the many facets of forgiveness. He covers this topic in-depth with the ability to provide both understanding for the layperson and the theological acumen desired by clergy. Having read this work, I've found my Lenten series for this coming year!

Rev. Randolph H. Raasch, senior pastor,
First Immanuel Lutheran Church, Cedarburg, WI

I first heard Dr. Paavola preach when I was in college. Relatable and authentic, he was a campus favorite. We didn't want to miss chapel if we knew he was preaching! He displays the same wit and warmth as an author. As I read *Flowing from the Cross*, I was drawn in by vivid images that explore the expanse and depth of God's forgiveness. Dr. Paavola's powerful storytelling and deep biblical understanding engaged my mind and heart. This book has been the center of meaningful devotion time for me and would also make an excellent basis for an interactive group Bible study. I found myself face-to-face with the reality of God's forgiveness in ways I won't and can't forget.

Jessica Bordeleau, MAR, author, speaker, and educator

FLOWING
from the
CROSS

SIX FACETS
OF GOD'S FORGIVENESS

DANIEL E. PAAVOLA

CONCORDIA PUBLISHING HOUSE · SAINT LOUIS

Published by Concordia Publishing House
3558 S. Jefferson Avenue, St. Louis, MO 63118-3968
1-800-325-3040 • cph.org

Manufactured in the United States of America

Library of Congress Cataloging-in-Publication Data

Names: Paavola, Daniel E., author.

Title: Flowing from the cross: six facets of forgiveness / Daniel Paavola.

Description: St. Louis, MO: Concordia Publishing House, 2020.

Identifiers: LCCN 2020012392 (print) | LCCN 2020012393 (ebook) | ISBN 9780758666833 (paperback) | ISBN 9780758666840 (ebook)

Subjects: LCSH: Forgiveness of sin. | Theology of the cross. |

Forgiveness--Religious aspects--Christianity.

Classification: LCC BT795 .P25 2020 (print) | LCC BT795 (ebook) | DDC 234/.5--dc23

LC record available at https://lccn.loc.gov/2020012392

LC ebook record available at https://lccn.loc.gov/2020012393

1   2   3   4   5   6   7   8   9   10   29   28   27   26   25   24   23   22   21   20

CONTENTS

ACKNOWLEDGMENTS

Forgiveness is the one gift we absolutely need from God. We might spend more time asking for health, wisdom, and peace. But we wouldn't be anywhere near God without forgiveness. Without forgiveness, we're His enemies and the objects of His wrath. But with forgiveness, we're His beloved children, adopted and saved for eternity.

But what exactly is forgiveness? It's an easy word to say, but it's hard to grasp. The Bible has many images for forgiveness, and six of those images are the essence of this book. We'll look at three pairs of contrasting pictures of forgiveness: Clean and Covered, Fixed and Far, Many and One. These six distinct images make a wonderful six-sided cube that reflects, like the facets of a diamond, the riches of God's forgiveness.

Thank you to all the people who have contributed to the book. Many students helped shape these ideas through our lively discussions. Special thanks go to Kelsey and Henry and their engagement ring and Katherine and her memory quilt. Thank you also to my fellow professors Dr. Nicole Muth and Dr. Scott Ornum for their wonderful ideas in chapter 8. Thanks also to Jamie Moldenhauer and Laura Lane, editors at Concordia Publishing House, as it's been a pleasure to share this project with you. Finally, thank you to my wife, Holly, and our children, who have made our home a joy over these many years.

Blessings to you as you grow in appreciation of the many facets of forgiveness. I hope that you continue to find new treasures in this one essential gift.

"When You Hear *Forgive*": An Introduction to Forgiveness

Kelsey trusted her ring radar. She was sure that if Henry came near her with an engagement ring, her ring radar would go off immediately. There was no way Henry and the ring were going to surprise her. In fact, none of us would be surprised. We all knew there would be a ring someday. Kelsey and Henry have dated through all of their years at Concordia University Wisconsin. They're a perfect match and have been just waiting for a few crucial words to be said. The only question was whether Henry could make it any kind of surprise.

I'm very proud of Henry. He did it! Kelsey, despite her ring radar, never saw it coming that night. On the third anniversary of their first date, after watching the same movie they had watched on that first date, Henry did it. At the end of the movie, as the closing song set the mood, there was Henry, kneeling, with the ring in hand. The radar never went off until that moment.

What joy! Kelsey found me in the hall the next morning to tell me the story and show me the ring. The whole campus has celebrated with them from that day on. The wedding plans are going great and the ring is as beautiful now as ever. That ring, which was hidden for weeks, is now on full display. What was hidden is now never coming off.

> **WHAT WAS HIDDEN IS NOW NEVER COMING OFF.**

Kelsey's joy sees that ring as more than just a diamond given with a few words. Each facet has its own sparkle. After a few weeks, Kelsey noticed that when she was sitting in the chapel at Concordia, with natural light pouring through the stained glass windows, the diamond reflected a color wheel of different shades, more than she ever imagined.

That's how marriage begins. You start so simply—two people and a ring that says it all between you. With time, the many facets of life together come out, each one with its own color. The good times and the hard times, the little apartments and the dream house all bring out different shades that you never noticed before. Your relationship is a simple stone, in some ways fixed and unchanging, but oh, the beauty, the shape, and the colors that are waiting to be found!

Forgiveness Is the Priceless Stone

Forgiveness is that stone. Forgiveness is our diamond of engagement with God. It is the heart of our relationship, the one essential we must have with Him. It's His bond with us that creates our relationship together. With the promise of forgiveness, we can come into His presence, and, covered by forgiveness, we can walk in His peace.

FORGIVENESS IS OUR DIAMOND OF ENGAGEMENT WITH GOD.

Solomon summed this up when, at the dedication of the Jerusalem temple, he described the prayers of God's people and His response: "And listen to the plea of Your servant and of Your people Israel, when they pray toward this place. And listen in heaven Your dwelling place, and when You hear, forgive" (1 Kings 8:30). Solomon could have asked for many other things. The beauty of the temple could have filled his mind. A greater measure of wisdom and the words to express that wisdom would have been a natural request. In the same way, so many requests fill our prayers. We ask daily, "Lord, give us wisdom, give us courage, give us health and long life." Our lists are long and yet still growing. But Solomon asked for our one irreplaceable need. Forgiveness is what God alone can provide.

Think of the sources we have for so many of our needs. I can find wisdom, or at least information, on my phone, and I already have more apps on it than I'll ever fully use. I can see the doctor to get a prescription for my pain. I can tell a friend my worries and he'll promise to go with me to the appointment that I'm dreading. I have help in phones and computers, friends and family. But forgiveness for all my sins—pure, immediate, unconditional forgiveness—can come only from God.

Without that forgiveness, what would any of the other gifts matter? Psalm 130:3 says it well: "If You, O LORD, should mark iniquities, O Lord, who could stand?" That prospect is frightening enough, but the scene grows darker when Moses describes such an accounting in Psalm 90:8–9: "You have set our iniquities before You, our secret sins in the light of Your presence. For all our days pass away under Your wrath; we bring our years to an end like a sigh." If I have to meet God for an accounting of my sins, what help can I possibly bring with me? No app on my phone will plot my escape. No friend will say enough good things to get me off. No pill will dull the pain of eternal death. My life can be full of good things, but God's hard count of my sins will dry them up and blow them away.

So, Solomon was right that there's only one thing I need to hear. Forgiveness is the one message we must have. When a man proposes marriage, he needs to hear only one word: "Yes!" Many other words will follow, but I expect he won't hear many of them. He has one diamond to offer and she matches it with just one word. He has the diamond and she has "Yes!" In that beautiful moment, their life together is set. So, we come to hear just one word: "Forgiven!" And with that, our relationship is set. Forgiveness is the one hard rock on which we can build the house of our lives together with God.

What Do You Mean Exactly?

After the young man asks, "Will you marry me?" and she answers, "Yes!" I hope that they keep on talking. It would be sad if all he said was, "Good. I'm glad we got that settled," and then they both began to play with their phones without another word. No, now's the time to talk. Let's have her ask, "When should we get married?" And he says, "Well, soon, don't you think? After all, how long can it take to get ready? And we don't want a really big wedding anyway, do we?" Well, they have some talking to do. How soon is soon? How big is big? Welcome to marriage, where you find that old words have new meanings.

So, what does God mean exactly when He forgives us? What is this relationship actually built on? The essence of this book explains six aspects of forgiveness in order to answer this central question of the meaning of forgiveness. *Forgiveness* is a challenging word to define and use. It can easily be confused with imitations and substitutes. So before we unfold those six aspects, it would be good to mark out what forgiveness is *not*. What forgiveness is *not* will give us a dark background against which we can display the many facets of actual forgiveness.

We have many false synonyms for forgiveness, appealing imposters that never match the truth. Imitation forgiveness is the cubic zirconium of a false relationship with God. But these flashy bits of spiritual thought, though promising much, fail to reflect God and His actions. Often, they say nothing about the price He's already paid. Instead, these imitations of forgiveness point to our actions so that they become small mirrors of ourselves rather than expressions of God's timeless love. These impersonations of forgiveness want the spotlight to be on our imagined goodness but never our faults. False forgiveness

> **IMITATION FORGIVENESS IS THE CUBIC ZIRCONIUM OF A FALSE RELATIONSHIP WITH GOD.**

sparkles just long enough to hide the shallowness of its promise. While there are many variations on these empty promises, we can distinguish three facets on this artificial stone.

THE PERISCOPE PICTURE

Everyone recognizes when you're taking a selfie with your phone: hold the camera up high, then angle it down toward you, and smile. But let's turn that camera just a bit. Instead of seeing yourself, use it to look over your shoulder and down the hallway behind you. Take that picture and you'll see the people you just left behind. That's a periscope picture—a stealthy look up and back to see what's behind you.

Our first imitation of forgiveness is the periscope picture. It's a mirror looking over our shoulder at the past. That picture of the past is not of ourselves but of someone else. Here, we hope that we'll be excused because of a comparison with someone in the past. You're not trying for a good picture of yourself but rather a terrible picture of someone else. You don't have to look perfect yourself. Just look better than the other person.

Imagine you're in a terrible dating relationship where sharp words and broken promises are the norm. But your boyfriend, if he in any way deserves to be called this, defends himself by pointing out that your former boyfriend was even worse. And he has the periscope pictures to prove it. He replays all the stories you've told of your ex, and he darkens them a bit with every retelling. When he's walked you through the periscope pictures of the past, you do have to admit that at times, yes, the past was even worse than the present. So your boyfriend argues that he might not be perfect—far from it—but isn't he better than the relationship you had before?

Is this the relationship you're looking for? Hardly. This is a shallow comparison by which someone lives a tiny bit better than his worst competitor and says, "See? I'm not so bad now, am I?" Who would stay in such a relationship? Would you plan a life with such a man? On your wedding day, would it be enough to say, "Well, he's not the worst man I've dated"? That's not enough. Settling for someone who isn't the absolute worst is not the gem you're seeking.

And so, if we want more from a relationship, certainly God in His holiness expects more in His relationship with us. He doesn't excuse us because we're just one step away from being the worst. Forgiveness is not a search for someone more guilty than I am so that I can say, "Well, at least I'm not this fellow."

Instead, Jesus' forgiveness deliberately sought the worst of men, not to praise them by comparison but to save their souls by forgiveness. He called the hated tax collectors, men like Matthew, to follow Him. Jesus assured the thief on the cross that he would join Him in heaven that Good Friday. That assurance came not because this thief was better than the other who was dying beside him. Rather Jesus came to forgive any and all who would, like the repentant thief, recognize their need and trust in the mercy of Jesus. Periscope pictures gloat over a sinner left behind in our past. Jesus' forgiveness embraces that sinner and keeps him or her for eternity.

The Insulation of Excuses

Forgiveness, then, is not a cracked lens held up to someone else's past. It is also not a shallow excuse that turns the view away from ourselves. When a relationship is going badly, excuses abound. A young woman might come into my office to tell me how things are going in her relationship. I get nervous when she tells me of another disappointing weekend filled with his broken promises. I get especially nervous when she has excuses ready—again—to explain his behavior. He was busy because he works so hard. His mother makes him so angry whenever she calls him. His boss has been so unreasonable lately. There's always an excuse. I hope that one day she'll finally walk into my office and tell me that they're through. If I ask why, may she simply say, "I'm tired of making excuses for him." Excuses can't save a relationship.

Our relationship with God rests on more than excuses. We might wish that God would, out of His infinite creativity, have an excuse for what we've done. Perhaps He could say things like, "She hasn't been sleeping well, you know." Or, "If only the bills didn't all come at once." And finally, "It's not really her fault. The children have all been so worked up lately." If God ever ran out of excuses for us, we would be glad to suggest some. Excuses are our winter gloves, put on in fear that God will rap our knuckles.

However, serving up excuses for ourselves is not a relationship with God. God won't cover up His anger under our thin excuses. His anger burns against all sins, and as we read in Ephesians, "We all once lived in the passions of our flesh, carrying out the desires of the body and the mind, and were by nature children of wrath, like the rest of mankind" (Ephesians 2:3). Sin is

> **OUR EXCUSES ARE JUST HOT AIR BLOWN OVER THE COALS OF GOD'S ANGER.**

our act of unfaithfulness in our relationship with God. We can't explain away God's wrath. Our excuses are just hot air blown over the coals of God's anger. Don't try to explain what you've done. You'll only make the fire hotter.

Eventually, we need something that shows both God's anger over our sins and yet also His love for us. He doesn't simply endure our sinfulness. He doesn't deny our wrongs and their assault on His perfect justice. No, instead of all that, God forgives even while He remains true to His own standard of holiness. Paul expressed this combination so well when he explained that Jesus was put forward as the payment for our sins, and "this was to show God's righteousness, because in His divine forbearance He had passed over former sins. It was to show His righteousness at the present time, so that He might be just and the justifier of the one who has faith in Jesus" (Romans 3:25–26). God allows the full anger of His justice to strike Himself in His Son, and by that, He justifies the world. Tired of hearing our excuses, God silenced them with the hammer blows of Jesus' cross and the quiet of His tomb.

THE PAYMENT PLAN

So, forgiveness can't be just a harsh picture of someone else or a thin excuse for what we've done. But there is one more imitation of forgiveness, one that looks ahead instead of back. This is the imitation forgiveness of the second chance. Forgiveness masquerading as a second chance uses phrases like "I'll let it go this time, but not again" and "We've talked about this. Now do better" and "How could you do this again? You promised!" The second-chance method isn't limited to only a single second chance. In fact, it relishes counting how many chances have been granted. It keeps a careful record of what's wrong this time, how it was wrong before, and how you promised that it would never happen again. Unlike the excuse giver who hopes to gloss over the pain of sin, the second-chance granter will recount and even expand on what was wrong and how it compares with what the sinner did before.

This accounting of sins gives an ever-shrinking window of change. It imitates forgiveness in that it continues a relationship. However, it is a relationship of debt and deadlines. It is a relationship where the supposed gift of the second chance puts the cost entirely on the one receiving the gift. Can you imagine giving your beloved an engagement ring, slipping the ring on her left hand, and then, at the same time, placing a payment plan for the ring in her right hand? Here's the ring; there's the bill. What woman would open her hands for this? Who would start a life together with the reminder that the first installment is due tomorrow morning? And yet, so often we think that this is the relationship we have with God, a relationship of the payment plan known as the second chance.

HERE'S THE RING; THERE'S THE BILL.

The payment plan of the second chance suggests that if we try very hard today, we can make up for yesterday. However, you'll never make those payments. That's the problem of the second chance masquerading as forgiveness. The interest charged on past sins is relentless. How can you make the payment for yesterday when all the good you might do today is required already for today? You can't take today's goodness, even if it exists, and put it against yesterday's debt. Today is completely indebted to today and has no spare change to give toward yesterday's bill. As Jesus said, "What shall a man give in return for his soul?" (Matthew 16:26). Clearly, no one has enough for that charge. Each day increases the bill, and never will there be an excess of good to pay down the debt. If God is going to solve this debt, He'll have to do it entirely Himself. He puts the ring of forgiveness on us with no debt left to pay. With God, forgiveness and our relationship with Him are entirely a gift, never a second chance to make a payment. God's forgiveness has paid the entire bill and given us only the gift.

THE UNFORGIVING SCALE

Among these three images—the periscope picture, the insulating excuse, and the second chance—there's no lack of imitation forgiveness. While these three are not the only attempts at forgiveness that we might discuss, they give us enough errors by which to appreciate true forgiveness. Our study of the six facets of forgiveness will stand out all the more compared with these imitations. But to appreciate forgiveness fully, let's take one more step away from true forgiveness. For that, let's consider the complete opposite of forgiveness.

Consider this one word: *unforgiving*. Consider the cold sharpness of that word. Make a picture of it. What do you see? Take in its glaring look and tightened lips. What epitomizes *unforgiving* for you?

Our digital bathroom scale is unforgiving. Our old mechanical scale had a heart. With the old scale, if I stood with almost all my weight on my left foot and looked at the needle at an angle, I could erase two, three, even four pounds. Have a bad week with the diet? The old scale understood and gave me a little forgiveness.

Our new digital scale has no heart. It doesn't care which foot carries the weight or how I squint at the number. It reads the same every time. And don't even think of getting off and trying again. That just makes it mad. It'll add two pounds just for you suggesting that it was wrong. Pick it up and try it a few feet over? Now you've really made it angry—trust me. Save your excuses and explanations. Our digital scale is a heartless tyrant. It is unforgiving.

> **OUR DIGITAL SCALE IS A HEARTLESS TYRANT. IT IS UNFORGIVING.**

Your scale is probably just like ours, but remember, it's just a scale. After all, it's just a number at my feet. But what's unforgiving can be more serious than a scale. Right now, I'm looking at what's unforgiving on a very serious scale. I'm writing this on a perfect May afternoon at Road America, a four-mile road racetrack outside Elkhart Lake, Wisconsin. The MotoAmerica road races are here this weekend and so the fastest motorcycle road racers in America are blazing around the track. Road America can be unforgiving. At this highest level of racing, the superbikes reach 185 miles per hour on the straightaways. At that speed, the bikes come downhill to turn 5, a flat 90-degree left-hand turn. Every rider knows the turn is coming. Yet, many a rider fails to make the turn and sails past the corner, either into the run-off road or, worse, into the gravel trap. The gravel trap is unforgiving. The bike will stop, wheels buried deep in the loose gravel, maybe staying upright, maybe lying on its side. Either way, your race is over. Turn 5 is unforgiving.

But turn 6 is even more serious. From turn 5, the riders power uphill toward turn 6, which is just over the crest of the hill. But the riders can't see the turn as they go up the hill. They have to know it's there, roll off the throttle, and hit the brakes before they see it. Forget what you can't see, and you'll sail straight into the corner, through the gravel trap and into the tires guarding the concrete wall. Hit that wall, and your day is really over.

Turns 5 and 6 are unforgiving. Miss either turn, and your race is done. Miss them badly, and your bike is against the wall. You can talk all day about how fast you were going into turn 5 or about how many bikes you passed going up the hill toward turn 6. But make one mistake in turn 5, and you'll be lucky to limp into the pits. Miss turn 6 just once, and you might be finishing in an ambulance. This track is unforgiving.

Consider how God could be just as unforgiving as turns 5 and 6. We race ahead in life, imagining that we're outrunning so many around us. We have plans, and look—we're really flying. But then, make one mistake, and it can all be over. It's just one wrong word, one hasty over-reaching, one sharp answer that sounded clever at the moment. But that one word could be enough. Like ignoring the danger of turns 5 and 6, that selfish moment could end our run with God.

It's hard to imagine that one sin could damage our relationship with God. How serious could just one mistake be? That's for God to decide, and He is serious. It was so with Moses, who struck the rock twice and, because of that, lost his opportunity to enter the Promised Land (Numbers 20:11–12). Saul hastily offered the sacrifice when he should have waited for Samuel. David took Bathsheba, and his kingdom began to unravel. Samuel sums up all such impatient acts when he said to Saul, "You have done foolishly. You have not kept the command of the LORD your God, with which He commanded you. For then the LORD would have established your kingdom over Israel forever. But now your kingdom shall not continue" (1 Samuel 13:13–14).

The judgment of God is even harsher than the imitation forgiveness of comparisons, excuses, and repayment plans. Any of our single sins is more than enough reason for God to say, "Go, be gone." It is as with the five foolish maidens who failed to prepare for the Bridegroom's arrival in Jesus' parable of the ten virgins (Matthew 25:1–13). Despite any last-minute knocking we might do, He could answer us as He did in the parable: "Truly, I say to you, I do not know you" (v. 12). Being unforgiven outside His door isn't just a dark day for the relationship. It's the end of the relationship. When we consider the necessity of forgiveness, remember the harshness of its opposite. If God is unforgiving, that's not a simple setback in our relationship. It's the utter end.

But the Engagement Ring Returns

Remember Henry and Kelsey from the start of the chapter? Henry had the engagement ring ready that evening. It was all planned out, though Kelsey knew nothing of it. I hope that that day was a happy one for them, when they shared a meal or two at the cafeteria, studied together in the library, and then agreed to watch their anniversary movie that night. That's the ideal. But no matter how the day went, Henry had a plan. Even if there was no meal and they disagreed on where to watch the movie, Henry still had the ring. They were determined to see the movie, and the ring was going to be there.

That's the nature of forgiveness. It was God's plan for us, long before we knew Him or what He had in mind. He knows the necessity of our having this forgiveness. Without it, we have no life but only a futile waiting for a final dismissal. But that's not God's desire or plan. Once again, we can hear Psalm 130:3–4: "If you, O Lord, should mark iniquities, O Lord, who could stand? But with You there is forgiveness, that You may be feared." We can go on to relish the later verse: "O Israel, hope in the Lord! For with the Lord there is steadfast love, and with Him is plentiful redemption" (v. 7).

God puts this ring of engagement, the diamond of forgiveness, on us, not because our hands and lives are pure, but because His forgiveness overcomes our stains. The brilliant light of His ring of forgiveness drives off our darkness. The cost of His payment is so great that our excuses are not needed. The fit of the ring is so perfect that we won't ever take it off. And while engagement rings are meant for only one person, this invitation of forgiveness is for everyone who hears it. Isaiah sends out the call: "Let the wicked forsake his way, and the unrighteous man his thoughts; let him return to the LORD, that He may have compassion on him, and to our God, for He will abundantly pardon" (55:7). God has put the ring of forgiveness onto all our hands. Now it's time for us to admire it and slowly see all its facets.

> **THE BRILLIANT LIGHT OF HIS RING OF FORGIVENESS DRIVES OFF OUR DARKNESS.**

IT'S TIME TO SEE THE COLORS IN THE STONE

I mentioned earlier that after a week or two, Kelsey might have noticed something striking about her ring. The urban legend at Concordia University Wisconsin is that an engagement ring looks especially striking when you see it in the afternoon sunlight that comes through the stained glass windows in our chapel. So, go to the chapel in the late afternoon, sit in the light, and turn your ring so that each facet catches the sun. What a kaleidoscope! What was a simple, clear diamond becomes a color wheel in the chapel's light. It's still one diamond, but oh, the differences you can see.

That's what we'll be doing in the coming chapters. We'll examine six facets of forgiveness. Our six qualities are illustrations of the single forgiveness from God. Before we see these facets, let's emphasize that there is only one forgiveness, which comes through the life, death, and resurrection of Jesus. He alone is the way to the Father, and His work alone brings forgiveness. The writer to the Hebrews says it clearly: "But as it is, He has appeared once for all at the end of the ages to put away sin by the sacrifice of Himself" (Hebrews 9:26). That payment was not the endless repetition of human sacrifices but of Himself. "He entered once for all into the holy places, not by means of the blood of goats and calves but by means of His own blood, thus securing an eternal redemption" (v. 12). So, this single payment leads to a single forgiveness that arches over all people for all time. Paul makes this clear: "All this is from God, who through Christ reconciled us to Himself and gave us the ministry of reconciliation; that is, in Christ God was reconciling the world to Himself, not counting their trespasses against them" (2 Corinthians 5:18–19).

This single life carries an identical forgiveness and new relationship with God to every person. Rarely do two women have identical diamonds in their engagement rings. If they did, I can't quite imagine them happily saying, "Look, your diamond is just like mine." But that's exactly what we do say to one another. "Your diamond is just like mine!" Each of us has the same gem, bought at the same price with the same promise of an eternal relationship. Instead of competition, this one forgiveness gives us the certainty of salvation. The forgiveness given to me is no less than that same treasure given to every biblical believer for all time.

"YOUR DIAMOND IS JUST LIKE MINE!"

Therefore, we each have the diamond of forgiveness. In this study, we'll see six different aspects of forgiveness arranged in three contrasting pairs. The qualities of forgiveness lend themselves to this contrast so that each description of forgiveness has an equal, opposite facet with it. Together, the pairs of facets make a complete picture. Here are the six qualities, grouped in pairs.

First, in God's forgiveness, we are both Clean and Covered, as we'll see in chapters 2 and 3. His forgiveness removes our sins by His perfect washing, which makes us new. But God also covers our sins so thoroughly that we need never fear that our old stains will be seen again.

Next, we'll see that forgiveness is both Fixed and Far, as we'll discuss in chapters 4 and 5. Forgiveness is centered in one place, the cross, and there our sins are fixed. Forgiveness is also the sending of our sins far out of sight.

Finally, forgiveness brings Many and One. Forgiveness comes with an endless speaking of His words, delivered with a crescendo of sound. The words of Christ for us have no limit, and they overwhelm any word against us. But forgiveness is also a still, small voice that says but one line, and that is enough. These two ideas, the many words and the one, are chapters 6 and 7.

As you can see, each of these pairs has an alternating balance within them: Clean and Covered, Fixed and Far, Many and One. By pairing these six facets, we can make them into a six-sided cube. Picture a simple cube with six plain faces. We'll put the contrasting pairs of forgiveness facets on opposing sides of the cube. In the end, all six sides will have a distinct aspect of forgiveness, and in this way, we'll have a simple reminder of our diamond analogy. Forgiveness is the engagement ring diamond with its facets, and our cube is that diamond reduced to six sides. I trust that the cube is an easy image to visualize. In fact, if you are using this book for a group study, it might be good to make a paper cube for each person and label each face as we go along. This six-sided study might work especially well with the six weeks of Lent.

Let's Put Some Life into the Cube

If creating and labeling the cube appeals to you, take it one step further. With six facets, we have a perfect opportunity to tie the cube of forgiveness to the six colors of the Church Year. Our liturgical calendar typically involves six different colors that are expressive of the seasons of the Church Year. White is for the celebrations of Christmas and Easter, while black serves for Good Friday. Blue in Advent reminds us that Christ came once and is coming again. Purple colors our Lenten season with the reminder that Christ the King went forward to the cross. Red speaks of the fire and power of the Holy Spirit on Pentecost, and green symbolizes the long season of Trinity, late spring through fall, and the time of our growing in the fruitfulness of Jesus' ministry.

Each color will be connected to one facet. You're likely already making some connections between individual colors and some of the clearest facets. I'll let your creativity go to work and will give you my suggestions as each chapter unfolds. I trust that the colors of each facet will help you see the essential meaning of that aspect of forgiveness and will also show the contrast to its partner on the other side of the cube.

If the Church Year colors work for you, then let's add another step. I suggested you make a paper cube, perhaps a core of rolled-up paper with six faces glued onto it. That works, but it's a bit flimsy. To be able to really handle the cube, make it out of something stronger. I made mine out of a solid block of wood and covered each face with a different piece of wood. Like the Church Year colors, each piece represents some aspect of the facet. The color and feel of each piece are unique and matched to a particular aspect of forgiveness. I won't give away the plan now, but I will let you start thinking about these woods: black walnut, hard maple, butternut, cherry, and red oak, with the oak being used twice: once cut in many pieces and then joined as in a parquet floor, and later, cut in a single piece with a cathedral grain. These classic cabinet and furniture woods are beautiful and durable, just like the aspects of forgiveness that we're studying.

Years Ago but Still Working

I saw Kelsey this week and asked her an obvious question: "Do you still have that beautiful ring on?" Of course, the answer was yes! Kelsey and Henry are doing just fine, and I expect that ring will be on her hand for decades to come. It'll be beautiful, shining with the same kaleidoscope of colors that it showed that first day.

Forgiveness is our engagement with God. It is a single, lasting gem bought entirely by God's work. It has no equal, though many imitations have come over the years. But forgiveness need never be upgraded or improved since it's the priceless gift of God through the sacrifice of His Son. Hold it up to the light and see the distinctive colors that it brings. Seeing these different facets, let's appreciate all the more what a treasure it is.

HYMNS OF FORGIVENESS

Hymns have expressed the truth of forgiveness for centuries. For each chapter, we'll look at a few hymns that capture the theme of that chapter. All of these are found in the *Lutheran Service Book* (*LSB*). If you are part of a group studying this book, you might use the hymns as an opening or closing part of your study. While I have chosen these few hymns and stanzas, you can certainly find more that express the themes of each chapter.

For the opening ideas of forgiveness, let's begin with "If God Himself Be for Me":

> He canceled my offenses,
>> Delivered me from death;
> He is the Lord who cleanses
>> My soul from sin through faith.
> In Him I can be cheerful,
>> Courageous on my way;
> In Him I am not fearful
>> Of God's great Judgment Day.
>> (*LSB* 724:4)

Notice the wealth of different images of forgiveness and the dramatic change in life that comes with the truth of forgiveness.

Another hymn that also expresses this whole-life change is "Chief of Sinners Though I Be." Notice how it shows that all people are welcome to hear the news of forgiveness:

Chief of sinners though I be,
    Jesus shed His blood for me,
Died that I might live on high,
    Lives that I might never die.
As the branch is to the vine,
    I am His, and He is mine.
Only Jesus can impart
    Balm to heal the wounded heart,
Peace that flows from sin forgiv'n,
    Joy that lifts the soul to heav'n,
Faith and hope to walk with God
    In the way that Enoch trod.
    (*LSB* 611:1, 3)

As we close this first chapter, please reflect on your favorite hymns that express the forgiveness God has for all people.

DISCUSSION QUESTIONS

1. The chapter began with the story of the engagement ring. A single stone and a few words are the foundation for Kelsey and Henry for all the years to come. When have you had a single moment that established a relationship that lasted for years?

2. The chapter discussed imitation forgiveness, including the periscope picture that compares us with others and the insulation that comes through excuses. Which of these two imitations is especially tempting as a substitute for genuine forgiveness?

3. Second chances are especially common as an alternative to actual forgiveness. Second chances sound like this: "I'll let it go this time, but don't let it happen again." How does this compare with the actual truth of forgiveness?

4. The chapter described things that are unforgiving—digital scales and racetracks. What else defines *unforgiving* in your experience?

5. We've used a diamond as an image for forgiveness. Consider the extreme hardness and durability, the beauty, the many facets, and the cost of a diamond. Which of these fit well with the actual forgiveness won by Christ?

6. One of the key points of forgiveness is that it is identical for all people. We used the analogy of engagement rings and diamonds that are identical. How would two women feel if they found that their engagement rings and diamonds were identical? And yet, how is the identical forgiveness given to all people good news for us?

7. The book will discuss the six facets of forgiveness arranged in three contrasting pairs. I suggest that the six common colors of the Church Year—green, red, blue, white, purple, and black—can be matched to these six facets. What are some of the pairings of facets and colors that come to mind at this time?

Clean

Remember bars of soap? In a liquid-soap world, it might be hard to remember an actual bar of soap. But let's go back to those days of thick, honest bars of soap. You can wash and wash with that one bar, but finally you wear it down to a sliver. In the end, it is hard as a stone, with the edge worn sharp as a knife. Still, you try to get one more wash out of it. But it's hopeless. Rub it, and it slips away. Scrub with it, but there isn't a single bubble. Finally, you give up. Reach into the cabinet and break out a new bar. Say to yourself, "This is new. It'll work." And it does. Isn't it wonderful? Wash up with a new bar, and you're in Suds City.

"This is new. It'll work." This captures the idea of our first facet of forgiveness. Forgiveness is cleansing. It's likely the most natural of all the images of forgiveness. We've certainly tried throughout our lives to wash ourselves clean. We're all Lady Macbeth in her desperate scrubbing, trying to remove the dark, murderous stain that she, in her guilty imagination, still sees. But despite all her effort, the spot remains. So, we can try to cleanse ourselves, scrubbing with an ever-shrinking bar of explanations, excuses, and future promises. But that bar has worn peril-

ALL OUR SCRUBBING ONLY CUTS US MORE.

ously thin. By now, its knife-edge is honed sharp. All our scrubbing only cuts us more. Our thin excuses burn into the wounds we carry. Our promises to be better just compound the failure that we've been. As much as we want to be clean, we can't do it.

We need something new to cleanse us. This is where we have to divide the world. There are two kinds of people in the world: welders and wasters. Welders are those who use the bar of soap down to the last speck. To do that, they press the old bar of soap into the back of the new bar. Somehow, they weld the two together. With that, they plan to get every last bubble out of the old bar. On the other hand, the waster says, "Life's too short to worry about that last bit of soap." Once there's an edge to that bar, he or she breaks out the new one. Don't try to combine the old and the new, says the waster. Life's too short to keep on rubbing. Get something new that'll work.

In this chapter, we'll rejoice over something new, something that actually works. God washes us with His own power and His cleanser. We won't try to combine our old methods with His. His cleansing works all by itself. His cleansing answers our natural yearning to go back to a perfect past. But it also addresses our hope that if we would be clean once, we could somehow stay that way. Of course, in ordinary cleansing, that never happens. But the cleansing of forgiveness isn't like our rubbing with a stubborn bar of soap. With God's forgiveness, we've been handed something new. "Here, use this," God says. His cleansing works.

The Stain Just Gets Bigger

Before we celebrate the cleansing of God's forgiveness, let's appreciate why this image of forgiveness works so well. I think there are several reasons why sin can be seen naturally as a stain. The first is that we don't plan on staining our clothes or ourselves. In fact, you're likely very conscious of the danger of a stain. Eat spaghetti and you'll be saying, "Don't spill, don't rush, don't make a mess." When I carry a bowl of soup filled to within a sixteenth of an inch of the bowl's edge, I chant to myself, "Don't spill it!"

But despite all our warnings, we still make a mess. We say that we'll be careful, and yet the stains are all around us. We can look temptation right in the eye and say, "No, not this time," and yet it reaches us again. Paul spoke of exactly this in Romans when he lamented, "For I do not do the good I want, but the evil I do not want is what I keep on doing" (7:19). Sin is a stain that we see coming but cannot ward off. The freshness of a new day is simply a clean white T-shirt that attracts stains the moment we put it on.

Of course, when we see the stain that we've made, we generally try to remove it. How's that working for you with the tomato sauce from that spaghetti? Or worse, how about the time you were painting the bedroom? There was that spot of paint that dripped onto the one square foot of carpet that you didn't have covered. Grab a rag or paper towel and start rubbing. Now how much carpet is stained? About twice as much as the size of the paint drop. Keep rubbing, and you can easily triple the size of the stain.

Sin might be a single drop that appears at first to be a small thing. But give it time and watch it grow. Sin spreads faster than that paint you're rubbing. Consider the many biblical examples where sin grows like weeds in a garden. Paul would have continued to persecute, arrest, and kill Christians if God hadn't turned him around on the Damascus road (Acts 9:1–6). David likely imagined that he got away with adultery and murder until Nathan was sent to confront him (2 Samuel 11). And sin is not content to stay with only the one person that it first strikes. Eve reached for the forbidden fruit, and Adam was drawn in almost immediately. From that moment on, sin has reached every soul. Sin, too, sets in when we try to rub it out with our explanations. Adam and Eve blamed each other and the serpent, but the sin remains. Our excuses merely push the stain deeper within ourselves.

That's the stain of sin that we see coming. We know the danger that's around us, but we try to ward it off. When we fail, we scrub away at the stain of sin and say, "There, that's not so bad." But there is another stain from sin that comes as a surprise. For that, check out my basement steps. Several years ago, I removed the engine from my Honda 750 motorcycle. When I got the engine out, our son Steve and I carried it down the basement steps to the shop to work on it. Trust me, that 750 engine is heavy, and it took all our concentrated effort to haul it down the steps. Being focused on carrying that engine, I never thought about my shoes. Our steps have an off-white carpet on them, and my shoes had picked up oil and grease from the garage. That oil didn't wear off in the garage. No, it waited until I started going down those carpeted steps. Carrying that engine, I was never thinking of my shoes and the stain I was leaving behind. But when I went back upstairs—oh no! There was no explaining away those footprints.

Isn't that also the nature of sin as a stain? Do you see the effect of every misstep you've made? Are you always watching your personal rearview mirror? Of course not, but we certainly have left trespassing footprints behind us. Have you tried to rub out those marks? They're more than oily smudges. Our trespasses are footprints set in concrete with our initials scratched beside them. We can rub as much as we want, but there is no removing either the footprints or our initials. When the sad, stained history of our missteps is so deeply set, what can possibly restore the path of our past?

OUR TRESPASSES ARE FOOTPRINTS SET IN CONCRETE WITH OUR INITIALS SCRATCHED BESIDE THEM.

It appears impossible. Stains set and stay. In fact, some are meant to do that. Woodworking stains are supposed to soak into the wood and color it. We just stained our outdoor deck this morning. At least every two years, I sand down the pressure-treated wood of the deck and restain it. I wish that stain would last longer. That is, I wished that until this afternoon when I walked away from dropping off something in our garbage bin. I was wearing my favorite polo shirt and it came away with deck stain all across the front. The stain was on the front of the garbage bin, spilled there when I put things away this morning. I forgot it was there and casually brushed up against it this afternoon. I can tell you that soap has no effect on deck stain. Desperate, I moved on to rubbing it with paint thinner. The paint thinner seemed to make it better. I've rinsed the shirt and now it's going into the wash, so let's cross our fingers.

Deck stain promises to stay around. That's what the stain of sin also intends to do. The stain of sin is like greed and its consequences for Gehazi, the servant of Elisha. Remember how Elisha cured Naaman, the Syrian general, of leprosy by having him wash seven times in the Jordan River? Despite some initial doubt, Naaman eventually followed Elisha's directions, and he was immediately healed. In gratitude, he wanted to give generous gifts to Elisha, but Elisha refused them. However, Elisha's servant Gehazi overheard and followed Naaman, claimed that Elisha had changed his mind, and received silver and clothes. But immediately upon the servant's return, Elisha, who had seen Gehazi's greed in a vision, said to him, "Therefore the leprosy of Naaman shall cling to you and to your descendants forever" (2 Kings 5:27a). And the result was this: "So he went out from his presence a leper, like snow" (v. 27b). The white stain of leprosy, an open sign of secret greed, had no intention of ever leaving. Hidden treasures and bald-faced lies couldn't ward off this stain. And so, the man who wanted the riches of Naaman was left with only his disease. The stain of sin intends to cover us completely and burrow deeply within us.

> **HIDDEN TREASURES AND BALD-FACED LIES COULDN'T WARD OFF THIS STAIN.**

MAKE ME NEW!

The polo shirt I stained is in the wash now. I'm really hoping it comes out clean. I can't hope for it being like new because it is really old. (I'm embarrassed to say exactly how old it is, but if it were one of our kids, it would be driving by now.) It'll never be new again, but I'll be happy with it being just old and clean.

But that's why the image of forgiveness is so natural to our hopes. In fact, forgiveness promises even more than we first hope. When God forgives, His forgiveness cleanses us to be completely restored. David yearns for this when he describes his sin and his hope of forgiveness in Psalm 51: "Wash me thoroughly from my iniquity, and cleanse me from my sin! . . . Purge me with hyssop, and I shall be clean; wash me, and I shall be whiter than snow" (vv. 2, 7). Sin begins early, as David says: "Behold, I was brought forth in iniquity, and in sin did my mother conceive me" (v. 5). Now, David wants to be utterly new. He doesn't want to go back merely to the day before his adultery began, or to a youth that was innocently remembered. He wants a newness that he's never known and a cleansing that endures.

Isn't this the wonderful appeal of washing as the center of forgiveness? God will see us and deal with us as spotlessly new. Paul describes this beautifully with the image of a bride. Christ views us, the Church, as His Bride, and so He both washes us and preserves us. "Christ loved the church and gave Himself up for her, that He might sanctify her, having cleansed her by the washing of water with the word, so that He might present the church to Himself in splendor, without spot or wrinkle or any such thing, that she might be holy and without blemish" (Ephesians 5:25–27). None of us could ever be faultless, so none of us would ever pass the inspection of God. But by the washing of Baptism with the promises of forgiveness in God's Word, God declares that we are completely clean, as nothing on earth could wash us. A bride hopes to be perfect in the eyes of the groom. But God says that He has washed us so well that He chooses to see us without fault every day of our lives together with Him.

But How Did You Do It?

My shirt is out of the dryer now. I can't believe it—it looks really good. I can't see the deck stain, though I'm afraid to look too hard. But I think my old friend will live another day.

I wish I hadn't told Holly how I did it. It would be more fun and a bit more of a late-night infomercial if I had just shown her the stain and then, an hour or so later, said, "Ta-da! The shirt looks great." She would have had to say, "How did you do it?" And that's the point. Why have a stain if it doesn't have a story?

> **WHY HAVE A STAIN IF IT DOESN'T HAVE A STORY?**

That's another aspect of forgiveness as cleansing that is wonderfully appealing. When God declares that we are perfectly clean, we have to ask, "How did You do it?" We're not cynical or ungrateful. It's just that forgiveness that completely cleanses us is almost too good to be true. We can barely believe it, and so we have to ask, "How did You do it?"

The wonder of God's cleansing is that God cleanses with the stain itself. God uses the very things and actions that are the center of the world's rebellion against God. He brings those actions with all their bitterness to Himself in Christ. But since Jesus needs no cleansing, He takes upon Himself our sins, and therefore we are cleansed by what strikes Him. The sins, which He never committed, were washed away by Him so that they no longer stain us or Him. His cleansing removes the stain from Himself but never returns that stain to us, who caused it. While Jesus' hands still carry the marks of the nails, those marks are a reminder of His love and the power of His resurrection. The One called a criminal is the cleanser of the world, the champion over the sins He once carried.

> **THE ONE CALLED A CRIMINAL IS THE CLEANSER OF THE WORLD.**

What is His method of such remarkable cleansing? It's a bit like how we washed our hands in the shop on the farm. All my years of growing up on our dairy farm in Minnesota, my dad and I washed our hands twice. First, we washed with leaded gasoline. It seems so strange to write this now, but it seemed the most natural thing back then. There was always a pan of gasoline in the shop waiting for us to wash up. Then it was into the house, where we washed up at the sink by the door. The green bar of Lava soap with its gritty feel was waiting. You wouldn't wash your face with Lava, but it worked great to scrub away what was left on our hands.

God has washed us through a similar process. He began with sin as the first washing for sin itself. Paul explains this: "For our sake He made Him to be sin who knew no sin, so that in Him we might become the righteousness of God" (2 Corinthians 5:21). You attack deck stain with mineral spirits and you wash off grease with gasoline. You use the key ingredient of the stain to remove the stain. God used sin to remove our sin. He didn't stand far off in stunning holiness and urge us to rub our stains harder. The stain of sin would only set in deeper. No, Christ stepped forward to become sin, to be stained, to be condemned as the criminal, and to be truly accounted by God as the bearer of all the sins of the world. By sin itself is sin washed away.

BY SIN ITSELF IS SIN WASHED AWAY.

But it was no gentle washing that removed the stain of our sins. Lava soap is gritty. The company will proudly tell you that it contains pumice that scours away your stain. So also God scoured the world of sin by the violence of the cross. God didn't cleanse the world with the airy swish of a magic wand. He didn't dismiss the accumulated evil of the ages with a gentle "Go away, be gone now." No, as John says, "the blood of Jesus His Son cleanses us from all sin" (1 John 1:7). Our washing took more than pumice ground from volcanic rock. It took the pummeling blows of the crucifixion. It took iron-hard nails driven into Jesus' hands and feet. It took the burial of God's Son

SIN IS VIOLENCE AND VIOLENCE WAS ITS CLEANSING.

behind the rock of the tomb. Sin is an angry fist shaken at God. But its cure was not merely an empty hand trying to flick sin away. The angry fist of sin was cured when angry fists clenched hard nails and hammered them into God's Son. Sin is violence and violence was its cleansing. God washes with the stain itself.

I Know It before I See It

Holly and I are cleaning the carpets next week. We go to the hardware store, rent the cleaning machine, and go at it. It's amazing how much better the carpets look when we're done, especially since they don't look bad now.

But I don't have to see the carpets to know that they've been cleaned. Just walk in and take a deep breath. Oh yeah, it's carpet day. There's that clean smell, that little bit of lemon, maybe a little detergent fragrance. It's all good, and I bet the carpet-cleaning industry has worked hard to get that smell just right.

What's your fragrance of clean? Is it the lemony citrus of a spray cleaner? Is clean the smell of warm flannel just out of the dryer? Or is it the crispness of cotton sheets just in from the clothesline on a hot summer day? There are so many smells that go with the reality of clean.

Is there more to God's cleaning than just the visual change? Yes, and what a wonderful idea this is. Clean is not just the absence of stain; it's also the presence of the wonderful fragrance that comes with clean. Cleansing takes away the old, but it also brings in the new. I might not notice the absence of dust, but I can't miss that wonderful lemon smell from the furniture polish. I might not see any need to wash the sheets, but that crisp spring air that comes in with them off the line makes for the best sleep. So also, the cleansing of our sins isn't merely an absence but also a filling. Think of how we might add this sense of fragrance when you hear the words of forgiveness. When we say the Words of Absolution in worship, we should open the church windows to a spring breeze. Let the promise of new life come sweeping in. We're forgiven, and that cleansing is the new air we breathe.

These are all familiar fragrances of clean—lemon polish, carpet cleaner, and washed sheets. But there is also another fragrance that comes powerfully with our forgiveness and the means of that forgiveness. It begins with the fragrance of the sacrifice that cleanses us. Paul describes Jesus' death in this way: "Walk in love, as Christ loved us and gave Himself up for us, a fragrant offering and sacrifice to God" (Ephesians 5:2). What a remarkable offering this was, and what an astonishing reception of it by God! The death of His Son is a fragrant offering to the Father. Who would have expected that?

Flowers are common at funerals. Beautiful bouquets that cost a great deal fill the front of the church. But rarely have I ever seen a widow breathe in the fragrance of those flowers and say, "Aren't these lovely? Don't they smell so good?" At the funeral of a loved one, the fragrance of the flowers is forgotten. It's a time of loss, not fragrant beauty.

And yet, the sacrifice that cleanses us, the outpouring of the blood by which we are clean, is a fragrant offering to the senses of God. How could God see the beauty of that day, even through the darkness of the final hours? Perhaps it is like what the woman did when she anointed Jesus in the week before His death. Matthew's and Mark's Gospels describe how she poured a whole bottle of very expensive perfume over His head. The beautiful fragrance filled the room, but it made some object that such extravagance shouldn't happen. What a waste, they said. But Jesus said, "Why do you trouble her? She has done a beautiful thing to Me. . . . She has done what she could; she has anointed My body beforehand for burial. And truly, I say to you, wherever the gospel is proclaimed in the whole world, what she has done will be told in memory of her" (Mark 14:6, 8–9). She gave all she had, a bottle of perfume that cost the equivalent of a whole year's wages. She gave it all for what? In the view of some, she gave a year's wages for a lost cause, anointing a man about to die. But it was no waste for her. She saw the beauty of His life and the precious value of His death. She anointed Him not just with sorrowful tears but with the fragrance of beauty.

I wonder how long that fragrance lasted on Jesus. Imagine the power of this perfume as she poured the whole bottle on Jesus. It must have lingered longer than just that night. I wonder if it was still there, just a bit, on Good Friday. Let's imagine at least that the Father was aware of it as His Son obediently offered up His life as a fragrant offering for the cleansing of us all.

So, let the most wonderful perfume you can imagine be part of your image of the forgiveness that cleanses us. We all have our favorite fragrances that say "Clean." Lemon polishes for your furniture, fabric softener for your favorite flannel shirt, the summer breeze captured in the sheets off the line—all those are good. But an even better scent comes with the cleansing of forgiveness. Imagine the most expensive perfume, poured out without hesitation, and given in generous love. This is the scent of Jesus' sacrifice, pleasing to God Himself and a fragrance that covers us also. God shares the fragrance of His Son's sacrifice with us, who have given nothing for it. The woman paid dearly to pour out the beautiful perfume that lasted a few days. But we have been cleansed with the fragrance of Jesus' sacrifice. In that fragrance, there isn't merely a year's wages but His entire life. Here is a cost paid only by His death. All this He freely poured over us without hesitation and without end. The beautiful thing the woman did will be remembered as long as the Gospels are read. But the act of forgiving that cleanses us and the fragrant beauty of that cleansing will linger over us forever.

It's Never Too Late: Even the Oldest Stains Come Out

Now that we're talking about eternity, let's think about stains and time. A child spills a plate of food on your light tan carpet.

When do you go after that stain? Do you keep on talking with the family and say, "I'll get to that tomorrow"? Absolutely not. The can of spray carpet cleaner is ready on the shelf next to the sponges. Get going right now! That stain is just going to set in worse if you wait. Your only hope is to get rid of it right now.

How does that work with the stain of sin? Is the cleansing of sin something that needs to be done right now? Yes and no. Often, we're unaware of our sin at the moment we do it. I certainly didn't realize I was putting deck stain on my favorite shirt. The child, I hope, didn't pick up the plate of food intending to drop it onto the carpet. It just happens. So, some of our sins happen without our plotting in advance.

But when it becomes clear that we're stained, it's time to be cleansed. That's the most natural reaction to any stain. Did you spill something on your shirt at the restaurant? You'll start dabbing at it with the napkin right then. So also, the stain of sin is something that immediately calls for cleansing. Look at the original sin committed by Adam and Eve. When they ate the fruit of the forbidden tree, immediately, their eyes were opened. They were conscious of their sin and their nakedness. That day, God walked through the garden, found them, and gave them the promise that the Offspring of Eve would crush the serpent's head (Genesis 3:15). The stain of that first sin would be washed by the blood of the One who both crushed the serpent and endured the piercing of the cross.

The washing of forgiveness came early within the ministry of Jesus, long before He bore the cross. The baptizing done by John announced that washing away of sin. "John appeared, baptizing in the wilderness and proclaiming a baptism of repentance for the forgiveness of sins" (Mark 1:4). Baptism, which in Greek means "washing," is a wonderful picture of this cleansing that comes to each one immediately upon Baptism. The promise of Baptism still brings forgiveness of sins, life, and salvation without delay to the one who is baptized. There are several biblical references to this washing, such as "He saved us, not because of works done by us in righteousness, but according to His own mercy, by the washing of regeneration and renewal of the Holy Spirit" (Titus 3:5). This washing is all His action. My favorite shirt won't walk itself into the washer. So, we're forgiven and cleansed only by the powerful action of God. This washing is wonderfully complete. Paul describes God's perfect cleansing, saying, "You were washed, you were sanctified, you were justified in the name of the Lord Jesus Christ and by the Spirit of our God" (1 Corinthians 6:11). Washed by God, we are clean from every angle.

A washing this powerful can take on any stain. David's forgiveness announced by Nathan is a good example. David had committed adultery and murder to gain Bathsheba as his wife. Those sins and stains were deeply set in over months. When Nathan confronted David with his story of the rich man killing the poor man's only lamb, David's anger was ignited. But Nathan turned that flame onto David himself by saying, "You are the man!" (2 Samuel 12:7). David was crushed with his guilt. While this would later prompt him to write Psalm 51 in confession of his sin, here, when confronted by Nathan, David said simply, "I have sinned against the LORD." Nathan immediately announced forgiveness, saying, "The LORD also has put away your sin; you shall not die" (2 Samuel 12:13).

This stain had set in over many months. When you have a stain, imagine letting it sit for a year and then telling the carpet cleaner, "Oh, that happened a year ago. I suppose it's time to clean it." I expect he'll say it's past time and too late. But God takes on the oldest stains. You and I likely have stains far older than a year. They're so deeply set, we can't remember our lives without them. But the washing power of God's forgiveness has no time limit. God's cleanser has no expiration date. When David cried out for washing, his confidence in God's cleansing had no restriction. He could simply say, "Hide Your face

GOD'S CLEANSER HAS NO EXPIRATION DATE.

from my sins, and blot out all my iniquities. Create in me a clean heart, O God, and renew a right spirit within me" (Psalm 51:9–10). Isaiah's famous contrast of our sin and God's cleansing has this same boundless, timeless result: "Though your sins are like scarlet, they shall be as white as snow; though they are red like crimson, they shall become like wool" (Isaiah 1:18).

What a wonderful confidence we can have in the cleansing of God. Stop living with that stained conscience and memory. Don't imagine that since it happened so long ago, it can't be clean. Give up on any remedy except the washing by the blood of Christ. It's time to trust the complete cleansing that only He provides. In your Baptism, He has already cleansed you. He sees you as His spotless bride and, by faith, you can trust His promise that He will always see you this way. Our oldest stains are gone.

So, Let's Keep It That Way

Your favorite shirt comes out of the wash perfect. The stain is gone. It's as white as it ever was. Now that it's restored to perfect white, will stains just stay away from it? Or will all that white cotton just draw in stains all the more? Scrub your carpet deep down. Do future spills respect your hard work? Or is a clean carpet just a magnet to every muddy shoe? It seems that the more you clean, the faster the stains run through the door.

OR IS A CLEAN CARPET JUST A MAGNET TO EVERY MUDDY SHOE?

Won't that same principle be a disaster for us in our relationship with God? If He cleanses us, won't the sin and its stain just come back all the sooner and stand out all the more? If our cleansing were left to us, yes. If we somehow could cleanse ourselves, we might hopelessly say, "Good, now stay that way." What a useless wish. But the good news is that God doesn't leave our cleansing to us. He washes us perfectly with the blood of His Son, and that washing carries us right to the gates of heaven. The wonderful picture of the saints in heaven focuses on the cleansing that brought them there. John was asked who the countless saints of heaven were, and the answer was, "These are the ones coming out of the great tribulation. They have washed their robes and made them white in the blood of the Lamb" (Revelation 7:14).

Here's a washing that endures. When we're washed now, we're washed for eternity. The standard of clean that God gives today through Baptism won't be found lacking under that bright light of heaven. What appears white today won't be a shabby gray in heaven. When God has washed us, we're cleansed to His own perfect standards. There will be no fading of that clean and no outdoing of it by what He has done with others.

What a remarkable washing this is. We will never be upstaged by someone who appears brighter. No hidden stain will leap up to take us out of the heavenly ranks. No new standard of brilliance will leave us trying to hide in the corner. We're restored in His sight to all the brilliance He intended us to have.

No Cover-Up Needed

It probably got to be a habit. You had that shirt you really liked, but then the stain happened. You washed it and that helped, but the stain was still there. At least, you could still see it if you looked hard enough. What do you do with the shirt? You could throw it away, but you really like it. On the other hand, if the stain is near the bottom hem, you could just tuck it in. Or you could wear it under a sweater. Then, just don't take off that sweater, no matter how warm you get.

I wonder if we don't often walk through life wearing cover-up sweaters. We're completely washed clean in forgiveness. But at times, we act as though the stain is still there. So, we cover ourselves with a sweater of frightened explanation. We defensively cross our

> **So, we cover ourselves with a sweater of frightened explanation.**

arms over our stains and tell the world, "Nothing to see here." We tuck in as much of our lives as we can and hope no one notices what's hidden. But for all our tucking in and covering up, we might still live in fear.

To all that, the cleansing of forgiveness says, "No cover-up needed." Stop hiding and denying. Be as the prodigal son when he came home to his father: he was determined to confess his wrongs to his father, but when he had barely begun his confession, his father welcomed him home, and the celebration began. The prodigal didn't need to hide his past that night. He was forgiven. What he had done was known, but his father's joy and love were even clearer. He didn't have to relive his squandered past. He had only to live in that forgiveness, which would never end.

Invite the sweater-wearers you know to come to this same celebration. Remind them of that simple promise of 1 John 1:8–9:

> WE CAN NEVER CROSS OUR ARMS WIDE ENOUGH TO HIDE OUR STAINS, BUT WE CAN FIND ALL OUR SINS CLEANSED AT THE CROSS.

"If we say we have no sin, we deceive ourselves, and the truth is not in us. If we confess our sins, He is faithful and just to forgive us our sins and to cleanse us from all unrighteousness." Help someone to face the stain of the past. But assure him or her that God's forgiveness is complete. That cover-up sweater isn't needed. We can never cross our arms wide enough to hide our stains, but we can find all our sins cleansed at the cross.

THIS REALLY DOES WORK

I'm not sure which kind of soap user you are. You might be the welder who gets the last bubble out of every bar; or you could be the waster, like me, who guiltlessly throws that sharp-edged sliver away. Either way, there's something wonderful about that new bar. It lathers up instantly and feels so solid in your grip. It just works better.

Like that new bar, there is a new and better cleansing in our lives. We can put away the useless sliver of explanations. We can stop hiding the stains that aren't coming out no matter how hard we rub. We are the forgiven people of God. The blood of Jesus, telling of His death at the hands of us all, cleanses by the violence of the cross. His blood cleanses when it should have left a condemning mark. His cleansing takes on every set-in stain and assures us that His brightness will never fade. Stop covering up the marks of the past. Confess and be clean. The cleansing by His blood really works.

HARD MAPLE—THE WOOD THAT REFUSES STAIN

As I mentioned in the introductory chapter, each of the six sides of the cube can be seen in a Church Year color and in one of six different woods. Let's make the first side of the cube out of hard maple. Hard maple is the wonderful tree that gives us maple syrup. The wood is especially strong with generally straight grain. However, it can also have wonderful swirls in the grain, and then it's often called bird's-eye maple. It's durable and easy to work with.

The one challenge of maple is that it doesn't take stain very well. Compared with the other woods that we'll discuss, maple's dense structure and tight grain make it hard to color. It's easier to just leave maple in its natural, almost-white color. Coat it with tung oil and let it shine.

Isn't that a perfect wood for this first panel? Forgiveness is cleansing. That cleansing, like maple, resists any future stain. That cleansing doesn't need embellishment or covering up. We are clean and that's all that's needed. The cleansing of God's forgiveness is a sturdy, lasting beauty that wards off any addition. Let the shining, clear color of hard maple remind us of the lasting cleansing by God.

White—What Other Color Could Say "Clean"?

I'm sure you anticipated this choice. Of all the colors in the Church Year, what else but white conveys the cleansing of our sins? White carries the image of the spotless, perfect Bride, as we read in Ephesians 5. White is also the color for our celebrations of Christmas and Easter. Those are the days that are central to our Gospel hope. Christmas white ends our Advent waiting and tells us that Jesus has come with Good News for all people. Easter's white greets us early in the morning with the joy of an empty tomb. The darkness is over. Only light fills His grave. He is risen to newness of life and shares that life with us.

So, put a panel of white on your cube of forgiveness. Think of beautiful white altar paraments, seen only rarely in the year but so welcome when they come. Think of linen, stiffly white, inviting you to feel how thick and crisp it is. So, we're cleansed to be His and always to retain the newness that He creates. We are forgiven. We are cleansed.

HYMNS OF FORGIVENESS

We can touch only a few of the many hymns that describe the cleansing of forgiveness. Perhaps most familiar is "Rock of Ages":

> Nothing in my hand I bring;
> Simply to Thy cross I cling.
> Naked, come to Thee for dress;
> Helpless, look to Thee for grace;
> Foul, I to the fountain fly;
> Wash me, Savior, or I die. (*LSB* 761:3)

Equally familiar and loved is another hymn of cleansing, "Just as I Am, without One Plea." Notice the satisfying cleansing in stanza 2 and then the range of all that forgiveness brings in stanza 5:

Just as I am and waiting not
　　To rid my soul of one dark blot,

To Thee, whose blood can cleanse each spot,
　　O Lamb of God, I come, I come.

Just as I am, Thou wilt receive,
　　Wilt welcome, pardon, cleanse, relieve;

Because Thy promise I believe,
　　O Lamb of God, I come, I come.
　　(*LSB* 570:2, 5)

Let these beloved hymns be the songs of forgiveness that repeat through your mind and heart. You are cleansed and loved by the Savior who shed His blood so that you could be His spotless child.

Discussion Questions

1. We started with two kinds of people. Which one are you—the welder who uses up the bar of soap right to the end, or the waster who happily throws away that last sliver?

2. We suggested that cleansing is perhaps the most natural image of forgiveness. What's appealing and logical about forgiveness as cleansing?

3. What's your favorite cleaner, either for clothes or other items in the house? How well does it work on both new and old stains?

4. We noted that the blood of Jesus is God's method of cleansing. What's most striking and unusual about this as God's cleanser? How can the violence of His death cleanse our stains?

5. When the cleaning is freshly done, do you resolve to keep yourself, your clothes, or your carpets always that clean? How does this match our own resolve when God has removed our stains?

6. The chapter described how we still try to cover up the stain of past sin, even when that sin has been forgiven. How would life be different if we fully trusted the truth of God's complete forgiveness and cleansing?

7. The chapter used hard maple and the color white as the wood and color that match this first facet of forgiveness. How do these two, maple and white, match well with the purity and the resistance to future stains that we find also in God's cleansing?

Covered

W hy did we think this was a good color? For our family room flooring, we chose a light tan carpet. What were we thinking? As you might guess, within a couple of months, there was a stain right in front of the sofa.

Of course, we questioned everybody in the family. What happened to the carpet? It was never quite clear how that stain happened, but I'm guessing there was an open Diet Coke set on the floor, an exciting play by the Packers, and a sudden celebration that left its mark. Some hasty work with a paper towel tried to fix it, but you can't miss the stain.

Naturally, we worked on it. Spray-can cleaners and sponges made it a little lighter. Next was the carpet-cleaning machine we rented from the hardware store. Work that stain over many more times than the directions say you should. Does it look better? I think so. If you tilt your head and squint, it almost looks new. So, load up the machine and bring it back to the store.

But where do you look every time you walk into the room? That room is about 20 × 20 feet with 400 square feet of carpet. Isn't it amazing how you zero in on that one square foot? You're checking to see if that stain is really gone. Wait a week after the carpet machine cleaning. How's it look? You hate to admit it, but the stain is back. Maybe it's a little less than it was before, but it's definitely still there.

What can you do? Just one thing: cover it up. If you can't see it getting clean, then you best not see it all. Pull that couch up a couple feet. Buy a rug. Get a little relaxed in your decorating and let a magazine or two fall there. Do what you need to do, but cover it. If you can't pull the stain up and out, then put it down under.

> **IF YOU CAN'T SEE IT GETTING CLEAN, THEN YOU BEST NOT SEE IT ALL.**

That's the good news of this second facet of forgiveness. Perhaps, despite all the promises of God's perfect cleaning, you're worried that your sins are waiting to percolate up and show themselves to the world. They might look clean now, but who knows the future? Maybe they're just waiting to come back with a vengeance.

The opposite of Clean, then, is Covered. Covering our sins doesn't mean that we doubt or contradict the complete washing that God has done. But it assures us that God understands our fears. He combines the two facets of Clean and Covered. We're assured that we're the washed, spotless Bride. But He also tells us that we're covered by His putting Christ Himself over us. We're clean in

> **WE'RE SAFELY HIDDEN, COVERED BY THE CLOAK OF CHRIST.**

His sight, and when He sees us, He sees His own perfect Son. We're safely hidden, covered by the cloak of Christ. David said it perfectly: "Blessed is the one whose transgression is forgiven, whose sin is covered" (Psalm 32:1).

KEEP THE CAT ON THE EDGE

We had a bad cat once. Raja was a complete mistake since he was a barn cat that others had tried to bring into their home. They failed, and for a reason I can't remember now, we brought Raja home. Right away, he attacked our house. He tore the edge of the carpet and the corners of our couch. Turn your back on that cat, and there he was, scratching away. Finally, enough already! I learned that the Sheboygan animal shelter will take a cat like this off your hands for a donation of twenty-five dollars. In the end, I would have paid four times that much.

The one good thing about that cat was that he did his worst at the edge of the room. He attacked the carpet, but we could cover that. Grab a spare piece of carpet, put it over the mangled section, and then set a bookcase over it. Covered! As long as the cat stayed on the edge of the room, we could cover it.

That's the safest, easiest way to understand the covering of our sins. It's our natural inclination when our sins first come to mind. Covering the problem is our reflex, perhaps even more immediate than washing. After all, if I try to wash a stain, that's going to take time. Others will see me working on it, and there's no guarantee that it'll last.

But cover it up in an instant, and it's done. Our first temptation is to cover our sins by denying that there is any sin there at all. "Sin? What sin? I don't see anything wrong here." How often we try to throw a blanket of denial over our sin and say, "Nothing to see here." The very denial, of course, contradicts our claim. If there truly were no problem, then let everyone look. But our instant cover-up gives us away. The faster I deny something, the more certain you are that there's something there.

That's the problem of denial with someone who suspects our sins. But how well is this denial going to work with someone who knows exactly what you've done? Our wicked cat was a terrible actor. Come home and take one look at Raja, and you knew he'd been bad today. He was plotting even in his sleep. You weren't sure what he had done, but you knew it wasn't good.

God knows at least that much about us. He knows the hidden parts of all people. John describes Jesus' knowledge of the world at the start of His ministry when crowds began to follow Him. Jesus was not deceived by any easy promises from instant disciples, as John said: "But Jesus on His part did not entrust Himself to them, because He knew all people and needed no one to bear witness about man, for He Himself knew what was in man" (John 2:24–25). Hiding our true nature won't work before the One who knows the hearts of men. John reminds us of this with these familiar words: "If we say we have no sin, we deceive ourselves, and the truth is not in us" (1 John 1:8). Denying sin is a bit like catching a cat. Our cat hated going to the vet. The only way to bring him to the vet was to catch him, wrap him in a towel, and put him into his carrier. When he was completely wrapped, all you could see was the towel. But one look at that towel and you knew something was in there and was working its way out. We can throw a blanket of denial over our sins, but underneath the denial, our sins are an angry cat, scratching and clawing their way out.

FIND THE CARPET SQUARE

If the cat has done its worst, you still have one hope. You have that extra piece of carpet, don't you? When they put in new carpet, remember how there was that square left over? You didn't throw it away, so where is it now? Under the couch, I bet. That's what you need on the side of the room where the cat attacked the carpet. Put down the spare carpet and it'll match perfectly. Set a bookcase on it and who's going to notice? Or at least, who's going to be so nosy as to ask?

Cover your stains with a perfect past. That old carpet piece is the carpet as it was on its first, perfect day. What a wonderful change it is from the mangled piece that lies underneath it. This is one way in which God covers us. He covers the stain of today with a perfect past. He hides us under the newness of Christ who is the perfect one, the exact image of God. Colossians tells us of the perfection of His image: "He is the image of the invisible God, the firstborn of all creation" (1:15). Jesus is the radiant God, who shone like the sun in His transfiguration.

COVER YOUR STAINS WITH A PERFECT PAST.

In Jesus, we have the complete image of God and the perfection in human flesh that we've hoped to see.

This perfection is God's covering over us. Paul describes this in 1 Corinthians, contrasting Adam and Christ. We bear the sin of Adam, but we will also bear the perfect image of Christ. "As was the man of dust, so also are those who are of the dust, and as is the man of heaven, so also are those who are of heaven. Just as we have borne the image of the man of dust, we shall also bear the image of the man of heaven" (15:48–49). Bearing the image of God was what God had in mind when He first made us to reflect His image. But that perfect reflection was lost in the fall into sin, as we now forever bear the weakness of Adam. What reflection of God we have is clouded by the weakness of our flesh.

But we're not covered only by the frailty of our flesh. In the sight of God, we're already covered by Christ. Our Baptism linked us to death—not the futile death of the man of dust, Adam, but the life-bringing death of Christ. Paul explains this: "Do you not know that all of us who have been baptized into Christ Jesus were baptized into His death? We were buried therefore with Him by baptism into death, in order that, just as Christ was raised from the dead by the glory of the Father, we too might walk in newness of life" (Romans 6:3–4). In Baptism's waters, we are buried that we might be raised with a new, perfect covering and image of Christ.

NEVER ENOUGH MEETS NEVER ENOUGH

That covering by the water of Baptism is a beautiful image. The water of Baptism that covers us is a balance to another image that expresses so much of our sin. For that, we need to bring together Proverbs and the Day of Pentecost as described in Acts.

You perhaps remember the lists in Proverbs 30 of three—no, four things that the writer finds fascinating. In Proverbs 30, Agur, the writer of that chapter, lists things that are wonderful in verses 18–20; things that cause the earth to tremble in verses 21–23;

things that are small but wise in verses 24–28; and things that are
stately in verses 29–31. Beginning the series are those things that
are never satisfied: "Three things are never satisfied; four never say,
'Enough': Sheol, the barren womb, the land never satisfied with
water, and the fire that never says, 'Enough'" (vv. 15–16).

Guilt is a fire that never says, "Enough." When guilt meets you
on Monday morning and burns within you all day, does it ever say,
"I've ruined your day, but now you have a nice
evening. I'll see you again in the morning"?
No, guilt rages through the night and wakes
you first thing in the morning. Guilt devours
your whole week. On Friday evening, does it
apologize and give you the weekend off? No, guilt is a fire that
never says, "Enough."

> **GUILT IS A FIRE THAT NEVER SAYS, "ENOUGH."**

Guilt is a fire both hidden and seen. It's like a peat fire, buried
and yet burning. The fire of guilt smolders deep in our souls.
However, guilt's heat and smoke still work their way upward, and
others can't help but notice. Perhaps our anger and the sharp-edged
answers we give to others are the fire of guilt breaking out from
deep within ourselves.

The people who may have known this best were in the crowd
of Pentecost. At the end of Peter's sermon, he stunned them with
this summary of what they had done: "'Let all the house of Israel
therefore know for certain that God has made Him both Lord
and Christ, this Jesus whom you crucified.' Now when they heard
this they were cut to the heart, and said to Peter and the rest of
the apostles, 'Brothers, what shall we do?' And Peter said to them,
'Repent and be baptized every one of you in the name of Jesus
Christ for the forgiveness of your sins, and you will receive the gift
of the Holy Spirit'" (Acts 2:36–38). How the fire of guilt must have
burned in them! They had killed the Son of God. This was not a
simple spark that flared for an instant and was gone. This was the
branding fire that would mark them for death.

When I discuss this text in class, I try to capture a bit of the drama. In a classroom with actual windows, I open the windows and begin to light matches. The sulfur smell fills the room. The smoke drifts toward the ceiling. Light as many matches as you want. Fire never says, "Enough."

Then I take a small metal bowl filled with water. With a new match burning, I say to the class, "Now watch, but especially listen. Guilt is a fire that never says, 'Enough.' But never enough now meets never enough." I plunge the burning match into the water in the bowl. It makes the most satisfying crunch sound. The fire is out. The water wins. I use a box that holds 250 matches. I ask students, "If I do this 250 times, which never enough will win?" Water, of course, every time. Water has a never-enough appetite and will gladly swallow up fire every time.

This is the covering of the fire of guilt to which Peter pointed. Baptism is the quiet water of forgiveness by which the fire of guilt is extinguished. The sulfur arrogance of sin is snuffed out. The threatening spread of guilt's fire is all contained in the basin of Baptism's water. Baptism endlessly encloses our guilt and shame. The beautiful calm of that water stands ready every day to receive our sins and cover them. Baptism's water never runs dry. No matter how long ago you were baptized, the words of Baptism still cover our sins, submerging them and silencing their threats. Guilt is a ravenous fire, but in Baptism's water, it has met something with a greater appetite: God's forgiveness, brought in Baptism. Never enough has met never enough.

> **THE SULFUR ARROGANCE OF SIN IS SNUFFED OUT.**

THE RUG NEVER LOOKED BETTER

The water of Baptism is a wonderful image of how God covers our sins. There's just one possible worry. Water is clear. Won't the sins still be seen beneath the surface? The fire may be out, but the scorched matchstick is still there. Perhaps we worry that our sins, extinguished by the covering of Baptism, might still be seen. Could we cover them with something a little more substantial?

It's like the problem of the stain on the carpet. Scrub it, vacuum it, and promise to never spill anything on it again. It looks better. But you're still a little worried that the day you have company over is the day the stain will leap up to the surface.

So, cover it with something more substantial. What if you buy a new area rug, a beautiful, woven oval that matches the couch and love seat? Put it over the stain, and anchor it in place by putting a coffee table on it. Now walk into the room, and your eyes are going to be drawn instantly to that spot. You'll be looking, not to see the stain but to admire the rug. That one square foot you dreaded looking at is now underneath the best-looking part of the room.

God does the same in covering us. He covers us with the life and perfection of Jesus. It's the record of Jesus that stands in our place. This is the covering of the entire life of Jesus, which is placed over each of us, and we have this covering through Baptism as we join Jesus in both His death and resurrected life. Paul sums this up in terms of an exchange. Paul says that his life was completely covered over, absorbed, in the life of Christ: "I have been crucified with Christ. It is no longer I who live, but Christ who lives in me. And the life I now live in the flesh I live by faith in the Son of God, who loved me and gave Himself for me" (Galatians 2:20).

We are covered by the entire life of Christ. He stood squarely in the way of any view of us. In order to cover us, He promised that He would never be separated from us. Our sins can't fly out of the past toward us. They strike Him before ever reaching us. When we're asked what good we've ever done, we can say, "Nothing." We've done nothing noteworthy, but the whole of Jesus' life speaks for us. Paul further describes this: "For as many of you as were baptized into Christ have put on Christ" (Galatians 3:27). Christ's whole life is the beautiful covering over us.

I know a wonderful student, Katherine, who is making a quilt from a collection of shirts and other fabric pieces that are important to her past. She's using mission trip shirts, summer camp wear, and maybe a blanket square from long ago. All these pieces are going into one colorful, diverse quilt. It looks beautiful. What a way to sum up her life and cover herself with her past.

The life of Christ is our memory quilt. Every episode in His life is a square in the blanket that covers us. Make patchwork pieces from every parable, every miracle, and every teaching moment that we know of Jesus. Slowly trace the edges of each piece and remember His words of power and love, healing and forgiving. Imagine the size of this quilt. If a three-inch square were made for every Gospel account of His life, would that quilt be large enough to cover you? Yes, every part of your life would be hidden beneath His. Look again at all the squares that tell His story. A week of remembering wouldn't be enough to retell what happened in each piece. As people forgiven and covered in Christ, we get to remember the squares of His life, which speak for us, comfort us, and forgive us. Some of the pieces of His life will be our favorites. Those pieces may be worn a bit thin, but they're never worn out. Regardless of how often we recall them, each of these moments covers us as His forgiven people.

THE LIFE OF CHRIST IS OUR MEMORY QUILT.

Remember how the bright rug covered the dull stain on the carpet? Remember how your eyes gladly saw the rug instead of the stain? How much more do we gladly see the life of Jesus laid over us. How much better does His life look laid over ours. When the rug was put over the stain, we set a coffee table on top so no one would lift up the rug. But with the covering of Jesus' life, we don't need to stake it in place. There's no reason to lift Him out of His place over us. We're covered by the calm water of Baptism that extinguishes the fire of guilt. Furthermore, we're covered by the whole of Jesus' life. No fault can be found in Him, and He covers us so completely, we can say again with Paul, "It is no longer I who live, but Christ who lives within me" (Galatians 2:20).

A Quilt of Darkness

The beauty of the patchwork quilt as a covering is wonderful. Throw away the flimsy coverings of our denials and excuses. Spread instead the whole life of Christ to cover your sins. That should be enough to cover us for a lifetime.

But you might still have a worry. What about the stains that live under the quilt? What if someone moves the coffee table and pulls back the rug? The stain is still there. When they see it, they'll know the rug was only a cover but not a cure.

So, what about our sins and stains? If they're covered, are they still there? Is there any cure in the covering by Christ? For that, let's go back to my favorite shirt, the one that got stained by the deck stain. As you remember from chapter 2, I scrubbed it right away with mineral spirits and then rinsed it and Holly washed it. It came out fine. I wore it to work this week and no one was any wiser.

But what if you're worried that a stain will come back? If it does, just more washing won't work. So, what to do? I've got the answer on the garage shelf. Come with me to the garage and see. No, it's not some miracle cleanser or some bubbling witch's brew of turpentine and lye. It's not a cleanser at all, but it'll take care of any worry you have about that stain coming back.

It's wheel-bearing grease. Wheel-bearing grease is the absolute blackest substance you can imagine. It comes in a tub a little larger than your fist. Take the lid off and look into pure darkness. Being grease, it's thick and will stick to anything. Once it's on, it's there forever. It's blacker than midnight on a no-moon night. Do you have a stain on a shirt? Worried that no matter how many times you wash it, that stain will still be there? Here, let's put wheel-bearing grease on that stain. Don't be afraid of it. Scoop it up, a whole handful. Use the whole tub if you want. Now rub the grease onto that stain. Cover every inch of it. Work that grease deep into the fabric. Have it come through on the back side. There—now hold it up and look at it.

Are you still worried about that old stain coming through? Not anymore! Nothing is ever going to come through that grease. That grease won't be washed off and it will never change its color. It's black, now and forever. That brown deck stain won't change the darkness of the grease. Do this with any other stain and it's the same result. Bring on your grass stains, ketchup, mustard, and spaghetti sauce. Cover them all with wheel-bearing grease. Work that black grease into those stains, and let it come through the back. Are you going to see that grass stain anymore? Is that ketchup going to show up next week? Never. It's black forever.

This is the final covering that God has done for us. We have gone from beauty to black. The richness of the life of Jesus covers us with His beauty. But we are also covered with the deepest darkness of His death. If we're worried that our sins will somehow escape from under the covering of His life,

WE HAVE GONE FROM BEAUTY TO BLACK.

then be at peace with the darkness of His death. In that death, we have the utter darkness that covers the world and our sins. No sin escapes this darkness. God covered the world in darkness during the hours of Jesus' death. Thankfully, while we live in the light, the darkness of His death still covers our sins today.

Now we have a new appreciation for a truth we've heard many times. We are buried with Christ in our Baptism. "Do you not know that all of us who have been baptized into Christ Jesus were baptized into His death? . . . We know that our old self was crucified with Him in order that the body of sin might be brought to nothing, so that we would no longer be enslaved to sin" (Romans 6:3, 6). The darkness of Good Friday is now our covering. We remember that dramatic moment when the light ended on Good Friday:

"It was now about the sixth hour, and there was darkness over the whole land until the ninth hour, while the sun's light failed" (Luke 23:44–45). The word translated here as "failed" is the Greek verb *ekleipo*, which means "to fail," "to die out," or in terms of the sun, "to be eclipsed." But Good Friday's darkness is no mere eclipse. Something much greater than a passing moon extinguished the light. For three hours, the darkness of the coming death of God's Son covered the world. The judgment of God against sin was shown with the blackness of those hours. Under that utter darkness, our sins were covered.

A Trip to the Fantastic Caverns

My wife wants to go to the Fantastic Caverns. Actually, adventurous woman that she is, Holly would be happy to explore any cavern, but the Fantastic Caverns are at the top of her list. Driving from Wisconsin to Texas to visit our son at Fort Hood, we saw dozens of billboards for the Fantastic Caverns, which are northwest of Springfield, Missouri. I have to admit that the billboards look great. As Holly points out, everyone in the billboard pictures is happy. I say they look happy because they're aboveground, safe on the billboard. But deep underground, let's see them smile then.

But Holly's right. We should go to the Fantastic Caverns and see what's there. I'm sure it's all safe, and I might even enjoy it. It's just that, left to myself, there's no way I would ever go into a cave. All I can imagine of a cave is that it's dark, it's damp, and who knows what's in there. I'll stay up here with the sunshine.

That's the difference between light and dark, being aboveground with the sun or choosing to go down into the complete dark. I'm sure that at some point in the cave tour, they turn out the lights to show you how absolutely dark a cave is. I would just as soon take their word for it and stay up here.

Despite that, we need to take a trip like the Fantastic Caverns for our last step in the covering of our sins. We are covered completely by the wonderful darkness of Good Friday. That covering takes us to the tomb. On the other side of the world, there was a cave that was truly fantastic. Into that darkness, they carried the priceless body of the Son of God. And into that tomb with Jesus, God put all of us with our sins. We were buried with Him in that darkness. Our sins were hidden in that deepest cavern.

> **ON THE OTHER SIDE OF THE WORLD, THERE WAS A CAVE THAT WAS TRULY FANTASTIC.**

God has guided all of us so that all of our sins are locked in the cavern of His tomb. This was not a mere one-hour tour. This was the entombment for eternity of all our sins.

The wonderful aspect of this cavern of His death is that the darkness is complete. Our sins are in the darkness of His tomb, but no one can enter it now. There are no mining operations, no excavations that will bring out the sins God has buried. No light is allowed in this darkness. What His grave holds remains forever in that darkness.

We can stand outside the tomb of Christ about the way I would stand outside the Fantastic Caverns. Yes, I'm sure there is a huge cavern there with many surprising things in it. But no thanks, I'm going to stay right here in the sunlight. And if a landslide covered the mouth of that cave and no one could ever enter it, that would be fine with me.

Furthermore, I'm not alone standing outside this cave. I might be the only one who doesn't want to go into the Fantastic Caverns, but I'm one of a crowd outside the tomb of Christ. Our sins are buried there. I don't want to go in to search for mine. And neither do you. Your sins are buried there, and I'm fine with leaving them there alongside mine. Let's all agree to meet at the door to that tomb and leave our sins inside. Christ went to that depth, bearing our sins there but leaving them when He rose. You and I can celebrate the light of Easter, the resurrection of Jesus, and His leaving the tomb. Let's leave our sins buried, your sins and mine, and stay in the light of Easter with the One who rose.

So, we stand in view of the tomb of Christ. There, in that darkness, our sins are covered with a permanent darkness. From the darkness of the cross to the burial in the tomb, God has hidden our sins beyond our sight. Take heart; we need never enter into that darkness. As we were buried with Christ, so we also have been raised. Paul reminds us of our coming to the light:

> We were buried therefore with Him by baptism into death, in order that, just as Christ was raised from the dead by the glory of the Father, we too might walk in newness of life. . . . We know that Christ, being raised from the dead, will never die again; death no longer has dominion over Him. For the death He died He died to sin, once for all, but the life He lives He lives to God. So you also must consider yourselves dead to sin and alive to God in Christ Jesus. (Romans 6:4, 9–11)

What a final covering is the grave of Jesus! Your sins are covered with the calm waters of Baptism, extinguishing the fire of guilt. You are covered with the beauty of the whole life of Jesus. Every piece of the memory quilt of His story has been laid over our sins. But we are especially covered by the utter darkness of Good Friday. His death permeates all our stains. His darkness defeats all the threats of our stains to break out. No stain of sin can emerge from the darkness of Good Friday and His tomb. Let the tomb be the final covering, the resting place of our sins. No one will tour the secret tunnel where our sins are hidden. They are covered in the depth of His death. As David said, "Blessed is the one whose transgression is forgiven, whose sin is covered" (Psalm 32:1).

Black Walnut—Beautiful in Black

There can only be one choice for the wood that shows God's covering. If hard maple with its almost-white color is the wood for the Clean side, then we need the opposite for the Covered panel. Black walnut is perfect for this. This wonderful wood has rich colors ranging from a deep purple to almost black. No stain is needed when the wood itself is so beautiful. This is the wood for special projects like awards, cabinets for your most prized collections, and furniture that will be around for generations. Accordingly, black walnut is one of the most expensive woods that is grown widely in the United States.

All of that matches well with the covering of our sins. The black covering of Good Friday is a beautiful mystery with a depth that needs no added coloring by us. It is a precious covering that cost God the whole life of His Son. What could possibly add to the beauty of such a sacrifice? Greater love has no one than the laying down of His life, and greater beauty and cost couldn't be found. So, let these first two sides stand as wonderful opposites. For the side of the cube that represents our cleansing, have hard maple, almost white and warding off any stain. On the other side of the cube, there is the deep beauty of black walnut. Like the covering of our sins, it is expensive and sufficient all by itself with no adornment needed.

Black—That Dark Afternoon Covers Us

Isn't Good Friday the most striking service of the Church Year? I hope that you have experienced Good Friday worship where you solemnly listened to the words of Christ on the cross. In our worship at St. Paul's Lutheran Church in Butternut, Wisconsin, we would turn out the lights in seven stages, one for each of Jesus' seven words. At the end of the service, the lights were out, the altar was bare, and we left in silence. Let the black paraments hidden in the dark be the color of Good Friday and the covering of our sin. Color the cube with these two complete contrasts. White is perfect for the celebrations of Christmas and Easter and for the reminder that we are perfectly clean. Black is for Good Friday and the covering of our sins under that blackness. We are forgiven—Clean and Covered.

HYMNS OF FORGIVENESS

Forgiveness as the covering of sins is beautifully expressed by the hymn "Comfort, Comfort Ye My People." Notice how the covering of sins brings a lasting peace:

> "Comfort, comfort ye My people,
>   Speak ye peace," thus saith our God;
>
> "Comfort those who sit in darkness,
>   Mourning 'neath their sorrows' load.
>
> Speak ye to Jerusalem
>   Of the peace that waits for them;
>
> Tell her that her sins I cover
>   And her warfare now is over."
>   (*LSB* 347:1)

Another hymn expresses the success of God's covering and the failure of sin's attempt to erase God's work. Notice this contrast in "O Lord, How Shall I Meet You":

> Sin's debt, that fearful burden,
>   Cannot His love erase;
>
> Your guilt the Lord will pardon
>   And cover by His grace.
>
> He comes, for you procuring
>   The peace of sin forgiv'n,
>
> His children thus securing
>   Eternal life in heav'n. (*LSB* 334:5)

Sin cannot erase or remove the love of God, but His mercy covers sin and its mark entirely. Let His covering be all that you see and remember, knowing that His work will never be taken away.

DISCUSSION QUESTIONS

1. What was the worst stain that you ever caused? Did you ever get it out?

2. Why is it that we instinctively focus on a stain or the place the stain used to be when there is so much of the carpet or shirt that is clean? How do we do the same when we focus on the stain of sins on ourselves and others?

3. We described guilt as a fire that never says "enough." How is guilt a relentless fire that wants to burn up our days, weeks, and years?

4. Baptism is the water that covers and extinguishes our guilt. How can Baptism with its quiet water and few words overcome raging guilt?

5. This chapter also described a patchwork quilt as a covering that captured many of life's best moments. If you had a quilt made from the best moments of your life, what would some of the patches show? If a quilt were made with patches showing the life of Jesus, what four or five scenes from His life would you be sure to include?

6. Despite your best effort to clean things, when have stains come back? When do we fear that the stain of our sins will come back and be seen by ourselves and the world?

7. The chapter described covering a stain with wheel-bearing grease, completely black. How does the covering of the cross and the tomb on Good Friday work well as the ultimate darkness that covers our sins? How might the burial and covering of our sins in the tomb of Christ give us peace?

Fixed

Our black Lab Keily was the best dog that ever lived. Loving and loyal, she had a special relationship with every person in our family. She went on countless walks with Holly, she slept each night at the foot of the bed with Nicole, and she absolutely loved going on Model T rides with me. Nothing is cuter than a black Lab sitting in the front seat of a 1917 Model T Ford. I think she loved me the best because she was never happier than on those Model T rides.

But one day, we found a suspicious lump on her back leg. She was already ten years old but was active and happy in every way. We took her to the vet, who said it was cancer. There was a chance that the cancer was limited to just that one area. If so, she could do surgery and take it out. More tests were needed to know if the cancer had spread. Of course, our hope was that the cancer was all in one place. Let it be in just that one spot. Then, with the surgeon's skill, it could all be fixed.

I know that Keily was just a dog and the idea of surgery for a ten-year-old dog might be a bit strange. But let's go from surgery for Keily to even more important issues. You likely have had the same conversation about yourself or a loved one. The tumor was found, but had the cancer spread? The doctors needed more tests. If it was only in one place, the surgery—and maybe the radiation therapy also—could fix it. But if it had spread, then there was little that could be done.

That's the theme of this next panel and the beginning of our second pair of images of forgiveness. Trap our sins in only one place, and then they can be fixed. It seems a bit dangerous to concentrate all our sins in one place. Add to that danger by announcing to the world where those sins are. But God has gathered our sins and has fixed them into one place to give us hope. Amazingly, even though our sins are not a tiny spot of our lives but have permeated all of our lives, God can bring them safely together and then hold those sins without any harm to us. In His strong hands, our sins are fixed.

> **TRAP OUR SINS IN ONLY ONE PLACE, AND THEN THEY CAN BE FIXED.**

I Can Feel the Difference

Our sins are fixed in one place in this third facet. The partner to this in the next chapter is that our sins are far away. Fixed and Far, these two images of forgiveness stress distance and the tactile experience of forgiveness. In the first pair of Clean and Covered, we primarily *saw* forgiveness. Forgiveness was the cleaning that resulted in spotless white linen, a perfectly washed shirt, and hard maple that won't take a stain. On the other side, forgiveness was covering—our sins being covered with Baptism's water, with the patchwork quilt of Christ's life, and with the deepest black of Good Friday. Clean and Covered, forgiveness is primarily described in terms of what we see, and perhaps that's the most natural understanding of forgiveness.

But now it's time to *feel* forgiveness as well as see it. Forgiveness is a tactile experience that reassures us with the permanence of God's work. Forgiveness is what we reassuringly find every day. We go to the same place for the reminders we need of the work God has already done.

It's a bit like knowing where your keys, wallet, and phone are. Every day I ride my motorcycle to work. My cell phone, wallet, and keys are in the left front pocket of my riding jacket. Every morning,

I check that I have them and that the zipper is closed. Do I do this just once? Before I tell you how many times I check that pocket, let me ask you how many times you would do it. If you rode thirty miles one way to work, taking thirty to thirty-five minutes, how often would you check that pocket while you're riding, just to feel that the pocket was closed and your keys, cell phone, and wallet were there? I've asked many people this question, and I've heard every answer I can imagine. How about for you? Is once enough? Two or three times? How about once every five minutes? Or are you like the woman who said she would check every mile, thirty times in thirty minutes? That's a lot of checking. I'm in the middle on this. I'll probably check on that pocket three or four times in a ride. I know that they're there after the first time—and I know the phone is there because it's playing my music through the speakers in my helmet—but I still reach over for that familiar, reassuring feel. Let's feel: phone, billfold, keys, and the pocket zipped shut. Still there; good to know.

I hope that you've joined me in doing something like this. You double- and triple-check that the lights are out, the doors are locked, and the computer is off. You double-check that the bills you paid online actually got paid. You resend messages if you don't hear back from someone within a day. You do this even though your children tell you later that they read the first message and you really didn't have to write them again, an even longer message, the second time. And while you're tempted to do it, don't send the kids a voicemail message to triple-check on them.

We need reassurance and reminders. Forgiveness brings us that reassurance. In this facet of forgiveness, Fixed, we're going to celebrate the aspect of forgiveness that is comforting and familiar. Forgiveness can be a dramatic change, such as when we are cleansed or when we are covered by Good Friday darkness. That change of Clean and Covered signals the thorough change that comes with forgiveness. But we're people who have been forgiven from our

Baptism on. We hear of our forgiveness every time we read God's Word. We celebrate that same forgiveness in every worship service we attend. Forgiveness is reassuringly familiar. Take this the right way: forgiveness is an old friend. I want my old friends to be the people I've always known. I want them still to love music and antiques, to live in Michigan a couple of miles from the lake. I want them still to go camping—in a tent, no less— every summer. It's all right when they tell us about a new book they read or the new carpet they installed, but please, don't change. Be the people we've known and loved for forty years.

> **TAKE THIS THE RIGHT WAY: FORGIVENESS IS AN OLD FRIEND.**

Forgiveness is an old friend. By no means is forgiveness boring or taken for granted. You love your old friends all the more for the years you've shared. It's the years together, the old memories you share, and the new ones you add that make the relationship. Forgiveness is that familiar friend, the relationship that reassures you of the unchanging God. He has fixed our forgiveness with eternal certainty. He invites us to be reassured with a familiar touch. I don't know why I check my wallet, phone, and keys so often while I ride. I know I just did that five miles ago and nothing has changed. But I like that familiar feel. So, forgiveness will always be held in one place, always inviting us to find it just where God has put it. Forgiveness is fixed.

DON'T LET IT FLY AWAY

It used to be so easy. On Mondays, the village workers of Cedar Grove would pick up curbside garbage. You could put anything on the curb and the fellows would pick it up. And people stretched the meaning of "anything." There was no load limit to what you could put out there, except it did have to fit in the truck. Ah, those were the days.

But not anymore. Now we have a pair of two-wheeled containers, one for recycling and one for garbage. That's it. There are no more sagging couches, broken-leg desks, or rolled-up carpets. If it doesn't fit in the container, it's not going. So of course, everyone fills those containers to the max.

The fear is that what you put out on the curb won't make it into the truck. The truck comes along and the mechanical arm grabs the container, lifts it up over the truck bay, and turns it upside down. It usually works, but not always. Let's say you fill it really full so that the lid is about halfway open. Then add the wind. Let that arm lift up the container and the wind really hits it. The lid falls open long before it gets turned upside down. Bring on a miniature tornado of swirling wind right then. Now papers are flying out of the container and down the street. Most of the garbage gets to the truck, but watch out for what's racing down the street.

That wasn't the plan. All that paper was supposed to go into the truck. But there it goes, fluttering away like birds just pushed out of their cages. Chase every page if you can, but the wind is faster than you are. What was together is now dividing and multiplying.

It's a natural worry. What if all of our life were in that recycling container? Take reams of paper and write the ultimate diary of every day of your life. Then stack those pages in the trash container. They'll barely fit. Set the container on the curb—and here comes the wind. There goes the lid, and the first few inches of paper are flying away. Let the truck lift it and turn it upside down. Watch the wind push those pages down the street. Race after them, but you'll never catch them all.

That's our sins, isn't it? We put our worst sins in the garbage container, promising that we'll never do them again. But sin also fills a recycling container since so much of our sin was done before and, sadly, will be done again. Depressing as that is, even worse is the fear of it all scattering. The recycling truck holds the containers upside down for only a few seconds in which the wind can blow things away. But imagine what sin would like to do with the record of our lives. Sin and Satan would love to upend our lives enough for each piece to fall into the wind. Imagine the horror of seeing every page of your life's diary fly down the street to be read. Chase them if you want, but even one page that escapes would be too many.

I'm Not Chasing It Down

As I said, I understand that the old method of collecting doesn't work very well anymore. It's more efficient to have one man drive the truck and never have to get out. The old method had two men on the back of the truck getting off at each stop while a third man drove. Also, with the new method, it's up to each homeowner to make things fit into the containers. If your stuff flies away, the man in the truck is not going to jump out and chase it down. No, that flyaway story of your life that you hoped would stay in the truck, that's your problem.

Couldn't this also easily be the attitude of God? The image we have from Revelation 20 of the reading of the record of all we have done leaves the burden entirely on us. You can't bribe God to skip over certain parts. You can't work out a balance, two good deeds for every sin. And you won't be able to ensure a private audience with only God listening. We can easily picture the crowd that would listen to our story.

So, don't imagine that God will chase down the flying report of our sins. Jesus warned, "Nothing is covered up that will not be revealed, or hidden that will not be known. Therefore whatever you have said in the dark shall be heard in the light, and what you have whispered in private rooms shall be proclaimed on the housetops" (Luke 12:2–3). This is our worst fear, our secrets broadcast with a bullhorn. Turn your sixteen-foot-wide garage door into a movie screen and play on it an endless loop of your life. That's our sin in its worst, most public display. The tumor of our sin, begun as a single cell of rebellion by Adam and Eve, has spread to every part of our lives. It is a cancer that can't be hidden or ignored.

Don't Drag This Out

When you have to face bad news, how do you want to hear it? When the doctor says that you need to come into the office because the test results came back, when would you like to hear what the tests said? When your spouse says, "Something's come up and we need to talk. But let's talk tonight," are you going to have a good day? Can you put that out of your mind for the next six to eight hours until you get home?

No, I want the news right now. If you leave me waiting and wondering, my day is ruined. Any problem I can think of will only grow with time. By the time we do talk, life is almost over. Then, whatever the problem is, it better be big. After all, I've worried about it all day. So, don't tell me that the neighbor's cat is missing and might be living under our deck. That's all? I worried all day and that's all there is? No, it's got to be more than that.

If you want all the news, then God can provide it. For an image of that, let's go to Revelation 20 again. "And I saw the dead, great and small, standing before the throne, and books were opened. Then another book was opened, which is the book of life. And the dead were judged by what was written in the books, according to what they had done" (v. 12). This is a scene that we might know instinctively. Somewhere, there is a record of all that we have done. After all, God knew all of our days before they happened. "Your eyes saw my unformed substance; in Your book were written, every one of them, the days that were formed for me, when as yet there was none of them" (Psalm 139:16).

What a reading that could be. If we say that it would take too long, remember we're at the threshold of eternity. What is time then? What does the length of the line matter? Besides, no one wants to be at the front of this line. As we've noted before, the warning words of the psalm would speak here: "If You, O Lord, should mark iniquities, O Lord, who could stand?" (Psalm 130:3).

But there is another reading found in the Book of Life, a reading that brings life, not death. The Lutheran Confessions identify Jesus as the Book of Life. All those saved have been written in Him. Reading this Book of Life brings the certain, unchanged message of our salvation. In the Formula of Concord, the contrast is made between the fears we have over our deeds versus the certainty of God's salvation: "Whoever would be saved should not trouble or torment himself with thoughts about God's secret counsel, about whether he also is elected and ordained to eternal life. Miserable Satan usually attacks with these thoughts and afflicts godly hearts. But they should hear Christ, who is the Book of Life, and hear about God's eternal election to eternal life for all of His children" (Solid Declaration XI 70).

The Book of Life that the Confessions describe is not the frightening record of our sins but the fixed, saving work of Christ. By reading His record, we know our forgiveness and have confidence. The Formula continues with this same theme:

> By this teaching, people are taught that they must seek eternal election in Christ and His Holy Gospel, as in the Book of Life. This excludes no penitent sinner, but beckons and calls all poor, heavy-laden, and troubled sinners to repentance and the knowledge of their sins. It calls them to faith in Christ and promises the Holy Spirit for purification and renewal. It gives the most enduring consolation to all troubled, afflicted people, so that they know their salvation is not placed in their own hands. . . . But salvation is in God's gracious election, which He has revealed to us in Christ, out of whose hand no person shall snatch us (John 10:28; 2 Timothy 2:19). (Solid Declaration XI 89–90)

What a difference this understanding of the Book of Life brings. We have gone from the fearful prospect of reading all our failures to the comfort of knowing that the Book is Christ Himself. His story we know, and our names are written in that story. We're the ones He came to find, the sheep He calls by name. We're the ones held in His unbreakable grasp. Forgiveness is being fixed within His hand. In His

FORGIVENESS IS BEING FIXED WITHIN HIS HAND.

hand, we have the familiar guarantee that comes with His unchanging story. Jesus gives us that confidence, saying, "Heaven and earth will pass away, but My words will not pass away" (Matthew 24:35). Our certainty in His forgiveness is secure, tightly held within His hand and His Word.

I Wish It Were a Different Story

If you're wondering what happened to Keily, I have to tell you the rest of the story. The tests by the vet showed that the cancer had spread. No surgery would work. Keily was comfortable and fairly active for another month. We petted her, hugged her, and gave her every treat she wanted. She and I took Model T rides right to the last day, even when I had to lift her up onto the seat. She surely loved riding in the T. Then, when it was clear we'd come to the end, we had her put to sleep. I know she was just a plain black Lab from the animal shelter, but honest, she was the best dog that ever lived. We loved her and she loved us.

I would love to tell you that the surgeon found all the cancer in only one place. Then, with a few sure cuts, that she could have taken it out. It would have given Keily a few more years, and I promise that we would have cherished her even more, knowing how we had almost lost her. Maybe you've had that sort of cure for someone in your family. The surgery worked, the radiation therapy did more than they promised, and the cancer was gone. Every day that followed was a wonderful gift of life that almost never happened.

It can turn out that way if the cancer is in one place. Sadly, that's rarely the case, both for cancer and for our sins. If our sin were in only one spot, perhaps we could cut out that one day on the calendar. If the reading of our life had only one black mark, wouldn't all the rest make up for it? But that's not the case for any of us. The cancer of sin has covered us thoroughly, as David makes clear in Psalm 51: "Behold, I was brought forth in iniquity, and in sin did my mother conceive me" (v. 5). We can't imagine that this is the case only with David, as Paul recounts the spread of sin from Adam on: "Therefore, just as sin came into the world through one man, and death through sin, and so death spread to all men because all sinned" (Romans 5:12). This tumor has spread to us all.

THE SCALPEL MADE OF IRON

If the cancer had been in only one place, I'm sure that our vet would have done a wonderful job with the surgery. She would have used a sterile scalpel and just the right amount of anesthetic. It would have been performed in a clean room with a safe recovery bed for Keily. That's how we cure things. We use the opposite of the illness. The cancer was ugly and unruly, but we would have met it with a shining scalpel working over a sterile bed.

But God cures with the illness itself. When the spread of our sin needed to be fixed, He matched the sin with the cure. His scalpels were the nails of the cross. When sin was so serious that cutting had to be done, God took up the hardest and sharpest tools of all. The crucifixion

HIS SCALPELS WERE THE NAILS OF THE CROSS.

nails driven into His own Son were His instruments. What a strange surgery by which we are healed! No antiseptic cleansed the nails. No anesthetic dulled the pain. No sterile bed carried His Son's weight. Nails, jagged and rusted, driven by mocking soldiers, fixed Jesus onto the rough bed of the cross, which He Himself had to carry. All of this is so wrong, but it is by injustice that God cured every injustice the world has committed.

This changes our view of the crucifixion. God is not passively accepting the death of His Son. Jesus is not merely the quiet Lamb who is led to the sacrifice. God is the one who makes the sacrifice of His Son. The nails must be driven not merely by callous men but also by the Father into His Son. Paul captures this with a remarkable verse: "And you, who were dead in your trespasses and the uncircumcision of your flesh, God made alive together with Him, having forgiven us all our trespasses, by canceling the record of debt that stood against us with its legal demands. This He set aside, nailing it to the cross" (Colossians 2:13–14).

The bill that stood against us is our worst fear. It is the fluttering record of all that we've done wrong. That is the record that, if read, would condemn us forever. That's the record we want hidden in the deepest part of the refuse bin. It is the last thing we want to escape on the wind, blown all over town.

But the record that stood against us has been fixed. The nails of the cross have staked our crimes to their own death. Because those nails brought about the death of God's Son, our sins and every demand that could be made against us have also died. When the nails were driven into Christ, the bills against us were lying between His hands and the wood of the cross. God's justice was fulfilled as our deeds were pierced.

> **THE NAILS OF THE CROSS HAVE STAKED OUR CRIMES TO THEIR OWN DEATH.**

This gives us a new picture of the crucifixion. I think we generally focus on Jesus being nailed to the cross by the careless soldiers. But there is also the intention of the Father at work. Jesus was the son of a carpenter and worked as a carpenter. His callused hands sawed and nailed for years. We might dismiss this as only a sign of His humility and perhaps His love of working with His creation. But what a prelude those years were for the finality of Good Friday.

He is the carpenter who carries the beam of His cross, much as He carried beams of wood across the shop each day. He is nailed to the cross even as He nailed countless nails Himself during His carpentry days. But now we see with Colossians 2:14 that God actively nails the decrees that spoke against us as Jesus Himself is nailed.

Now our sins are fixed. They are captured for all time in this one place. The decrees that would have described our sins and would have loved to be broadcast on every corner, those decrees are no longer free. They are themselves nailed to the cross. Remember our fear about the contents of our overflowing recycling bin being blown throughout the town? The scattering of our sin and the advertising of the judgment against us would have been much worse than that. But now those sins are utterly captured. They are arrested not merely by the thin plastic of a recycling container with its floppy lid. No, let's take a deep, contented breath of relief. Our sins are held by the nails of the cross driven deep, deep into the wood.

The Pole Barn Nails

Picture those nails that hold the decree that would speak against you. How do you see those nails? When I was a boy, my father used what we called pole barn nails to build sheds and small buildings on the farm. They were longer and thicker than the common sixteen-penny nails used to join two-by-four lumber. I couldn't drive those pole barn nails very well, but Dad could. He never missed with his hammer and never hesitated. Five or six strokes and that nail was in, set deeply below the surface of the wood. The pole barn nails had rings around the nail near the head, and those rings resisted any attempt to pull the nail out again. Picture those nails being used to hold your sins on the cross. The head of the nail is sunk deep and it cannot be pulled up. What God has driven in cannot be undone.

What God has driven in cannot be undone.

This nailing fixes our sins in place and stops them from ever threatening us again. Remember how we began the chapter by speaking of our desire for the cancer to be fixed in one spot? That wish has come true for our spiritual cancer. The nails of the cross have located and fixed our sins and the decree against them in that one place: on the cross. We have the relief of knowing they remain in one familiar place.

What a victory this is over sin! Usually, we fear the record of our sins, and we stay as far from that record as possible. But when our sins are fixed by the cross and its nails, then they have lost their power. Our sins are trapped, but we're now free. Formerly, we hid from the judgment upon sin. But now the cross and its nails draw us forward. We can stand together fearlessly at the cross. The power of sin and the threatening broadcast of our crimes has ended. A stake has been driven through the power of sin.

And we might still see those nails. Here is when we want to have that familiar, reassuring touch—but don't just feel your pocket for your billfold or phone. Instead, imagine feeling the nails of the cross. Feel the depth of their being driven. For reassurance, imagine running your hand over the rough wood of the cross—there the nails still are, deeply set in that wood. That wood won't decay or split and those nails won't ever come out. Go there every day for that ever-sturdy reassurance. Your sins are fixed.

That Makes It Hard to See

Our town has a wonderful summer festival called Hollandfest, celebrating Cedar Grove's Dutch heritage. On Saturday morning, more than five hundred people race either the two-mile or the ten-kilometer race. At the end of the races, the results are posted on a board with the top ten finishers in each class. With two races and divisions for men and women divided by age groups of ten years, there are two to three hundred names listed in small print. There is a rope barrier that keeps everyone at least ten feet away.

Remember that last tiny line the eye doctor has you try to read in your eye exam? The eye exam print is huge compared to reading the results board at Hollandfest. We all crowd around, squint, and guess together who was in seventh place in the men's forty to forty-nine-year-old class for the 10K.

Now imagine if the organizers did this differently. Let's have someone complain a bit too loudly that they can't see, and also that it's taking too long. Let the volunteers who are kindly doing this out of the goodness of their hearts take offense. You want results? You want them right now? Fine. Here, take all the result sheets. Let's shuffle them all together, men and women, two-mile and 10K, some upside down, some backward. You want results? *Here.* And with that, the head official picks up the stack of results and drives a nail through them all, staking them onto that result board. There. Good luck reading *that!*

Of course, the kind, efficient people of the festival would never do that. It would be impossible to see the results. You could never see how anyone did. Squint all you want, lean up against that rope, and ask one another what you see. Nothing will work. The results are there, but no one will ever read them.

THE RESULTS ARE THERE, BUT NO ONE WILL EVER READ THEM.

That's how our sins are fixed. God has taken the results of the world, stacked and shuffled them together, and fixed them into one place with the nails of the cross. Imagine what billions of names crowded together look like if they could ever be printed together. How tiny is the print just for the names? Add the decrees that stand against each of us and the print is even smaller. And let the names be shuffled—no twenty-first-century English alphabetic order here.

Crowd together as much as you like. Look up to the crossbar where the records are held. Those nails are well past our reach. No one can climb up there to read better. Ask one another, "Can you see anything?" The wonderful answer is "No." No—the decrees are all there, but we can't get any closer. The print won't get bigger. The names won't follow any alphabet you know. The decree that stood against you is there, but neither you nor anyone else will read it. Your record is there, but the nails will never let it go.

YOUR RECORD IS THERE, BUT THE NAILS WILL NEVER LET IT GO.

As hard as we might strain to read the record, there is only one line that can be read from the cross. Pilate had ordered that the announcement be nailed above Jesus' head in Aramaic, Latin, and Greek: "Jesus of Nazareth, the King of the Jews" (see John 19:19–20). This title could be read by everyone who walked by, and this became the complaint of the chief priests, who wanted it changed to read, "This man said, 'I am King of the Jews.'" But Pilate answered, "What I have written I have written" (vv. 21–22).

What a perfect contrast. The charges that stand against us cannot be read, as they're stacked under the nails. But the one line the world has never forgotten is this: Jesus of Nazareth, King of the Jews. Yes, what Pilate has written remains written and read by the world. Our record is buried beneath the nails, which will never be moved. The King has put His name and title over all, and that alone will be read on the cross.

In Only One Place

If only Keily's tumor had contained all the cancer, she might have had several more years with us. Of course, she was already an older dog with her black face turning to white, so those years would have been few. But we would have been glad to pay the surgeon to take that single tumor out to gain those years.

What a wonderful difference for us. Our sins should have been spread not only through our lives but also scattered to our shame. Instead, they are now in only one place. God has imprisoned them under the nails of the cross. The scalpel that heals is the deadly nail of the cross. Under the nails of the cross, all our names and all the

THE SCALPEL THAT HEALS IS THE DEADLY NAIL OF THE CROSS.

charges against us are gathered, shuffled, and trapped. Let the world crowd near. No one can read those charges and names because the nail holds them at a distance that is safe for us. The one thing we can read is the truth about the Carpenter. His callused hands well knew nails and hammers, and His title remains the only line the world can read: "Jesus of Nazareth, King of the Jews." The Carpenter King has captured our sins under the nails of His cross. Our sins are fixed.

CHERRY—THE COLOR DEEPENS EVERY YEAR

Cherry is the wood that changes. The change is not one of structure or strength. Cherry is a stable, relatively strong wood that is often used for fine furniture and cabinets. Its tight grain is easy to saw, shape, and sand. Once built, cherry furniture has every reason to last for generations.

Yet, for all its permanence, cherry changes. When it is first sawn, cherry boards are light brown with little natural attraction. But over time, when exposed to the sun, cherry turns a deep red color. No stain is needed. Time alone will bring out the wonderful color. I built a cherry side table ten years ago and made another one to match this past year. Oh, the difference in the color between these two otherwise-identical tables. The new one is still fairly plain tan with only a hint of red, while the old one is the deep red for which cherry is loved.

Isn't this the color we expect of the cross? Perhaps the whole cross should be cherry so that the beauty of the cross would deepen each year. Wouldn't that be a marvelous goal for each Lenten season? May each Lent bring us a deeper hue of red, an echo of the purple of Good Friday's robe and a reminder that the nails will bring the deepest red as His blood is shed. Cherry can be nailed when driven by a strong hand. So, let the nails be driven deep into this wood, and let its red color grow to remind of us of the sacrifice of the King.

PURPLE—THE KING TAKES THE TITLE

Lent brings us the somber, rich color purple for the six-week journey to the cross. As we gather each year, we watch in wonder that the Carpenter and Teacher from Nazareth becomes the King acclaimed on Palm Sunday. But He gives away the honor that He could have demanded. In mockery, a purple robe is put upon Him as the soldiers call to Him, "Hail, King of the Jews!" (see John 19:1–3).

The robe was soon stripped away, and the mocking laughter likely died when darkness settled over the world for His final three hours. But two things endured: the nails of the cross held Him for the whole six hours, and the title "King of the Jews" lasts still today. Our names and the record of our sins are staked, hidden under the work of the King. What notice would anyone give to our deeds when the Son of God is laid over them? Our names and deeds are safely fixed beneath the nails when the King chooses to die for the world.

HYMNS OF FORGIVENESS

This chapter focuses on sins being entirely fixed on the cross. This idea is perfectly expressed by "When Peace, like a River." Notice the relief that comes when all of our sin is immovably nailed to the cross:

> He lives—oh, the bliss of this glorious
> thought;
> My sin, not in part, but the whole, Is nailed
> to His cross, and I bear it no more.
> Praise the Lord, praise the Lord, O my soul!
> It is well with my soul, It is well, it is well
> with my soul. (*LSB* 763:3)

While our sins are carried by the nails of the cross, we might see something else written upon the cross. The hymn "We Sing the Praise of Him Who Died" has us see the message of God's love inscribed on the cross:

> Inscribed upon the cross we see
>   In shining letters, "God is love."
>
> He bears our sins upon the tree;
>   He brings us mercy from above.
>   (*LSB* 429:2)

The nails of the cross hold all our sins and will not let them go. The only words that come from the cross are the words of His forgiveness and love. There, our sins are fixed forever by His nails.

Discussion Questions

1. We began the chapter with the story of Keily and our hope that all that was wrong with her would be in only one place. When have you had the same hope that all that was wrong would be centered in just one place?

2. I wrote of my tendency to recheck my keys, wallet, and phone while I ride. When do you check and recheck what's important? How does this also match with our need to be reassured about the most important matter, forgiveness of sins?

3. Our recycling and garbage containers are often full to the top. Don't let the wind blow the lid off! How is this a picture of our fear that our sins might be blown throughout the town? You might use the record of our lives as pictured with the Book of Life in Revelation 20.

4. We fear the scattering of our sins, but God's answer is the opposite. Instead of sending the record against us out of sight, God traps them in plain sight on the cross. How is it a relief that our sins cannot escape the cross?

5. We would have been happy to have the surgeon cure Keily with an antiseptic scalpel. God cured the entire world with the rough cruelty of the nails of the cross. Why would God use the injustice and violence of the cross to fix our sins?

6. Like the results of a race, we can imagine the decrees that speak against us being stacked up and nailed onto the cross. They are in plain sight, yet they can't be read. They are many, but they are completely trapped. How is this the wonderful result of Christ's sacrifice as the King of the Jews?

7. Dark cherry wood and the color purple are the images for this panel on the cube. With this facet of forgiveness, we focus on the cross and its nails. Why are dark cherry and purple good expressions of our sins being fixed on the cross?

Far

We're moving! After twenty-three years in our house in Cedar Grove, Holly and I are moving this summer. We're as surprised at this as anyone. Our neighbors say they thought we would never leave. (We're hoping they mean that in a good way.) But we're not going far. Staying in Cedar Grove, we're going from the northwest edge of town to the south end of Main Street. When people ask why we're moving, I tell them that I can't take those northern winters anymore.

Moving is a lot of work. This is the eighth move in our forty years of marriage. But twenty-three years in one place means we've got a lot of stuff. Holly is the champion of filling boxes, marking, and sealing. That ripping sound of packing tape fills the house. We know all our stuff is still here somewhere. It's just a question of which box it's in.

So, why go through all this? It's not because of our neighbors, I guarantee you. We have absolutely wonderful neighbors whom we will miss very much. But for others—not us—getting away from the neighborhood can be the reason for a move. You can call it the geographical cure. It's the hope that your troubles will disappear when you change your geography. Do you have a neighbor who makes you dread coming home? You've talked to him but nothing changes. In fact, since you brought it up, things have only gotten worse. Also, your son has started spending way too much time with the two boys down the block who make you worry. The more you try to steer him away from them, the more he ends up at their house.

What do you do? Move. Doesn't that sound like the cure? Open up those online realty sites, tour some houses, and take the plunge. Pack up and put the problem behind you. It's a ton of work, but you can't live like you are now.

The geographical cure is so attractive when you're surrounded by trouble. If the problems won't change, you can't stay. It seems there's only one thing to do: move. I'm not saying this is a wise step, but I think we can all understand the attraction. When your troubles are at your elbow every day and they're only getting worse, someone's going to have to move. Ideally, your problem people would be the ones to move. Wouldn't it be great to wake up one morning and see a U-Haul truck parked in their driveway? If that happened, you'd help them load. But that won't happen. No, when trouble lives next door, the moving truck ends up in your driveway.

WHEN TROUBLE LIVES NEXT DOOR, THE MOVING TRUCK ENDS UP IN YOUR DRIVEWAY.

That's the attraction of our next facet of forgiveness. We've been given the courage to gather at the cross, where our sins are fixed by the nails of Good Friday. We stand in faith that the decrees that stood against us are forever locked in place and rendered unreadable by the nails. We can't even see the charges against us, and God has chosen not to read them because the one sign that matters is "Jesus of Nazareth, King of the Jews." Our sins are in plain sight, but the nails of the cross have fixed them.

Despite that, wouldn't it be good to have our sins far away? I appreciate the bold reassurance that comes from the nails of the cross, but my natural inclination is to put some distance between my sins and me. Couldn't I try the geographical cure? Sin has settled in like a bad next-door neighbor, and I want to move.

Of course, there's a problem with this solution. In the geographical cure, you can move and your old neighbors will stay behind. But you might find that their identical twins live next door to your new house. You can move again, but their cousins will be there ahead of you.

But we have a wonderful answer to that in the forgiveness of sins. God remarkably sends our sins far away while we get to remain firmly home with Him. Sin moves, but we don't have to follow. And even better, our sins aren't coming back because they've gone to their death. Here is a wonderful thought: tell your sins it's time they moved and never come back. Forgiveness has this wonderful truth: our sins have been taken far away.

TELL YOUR SINS IT'S TIME THEY MOVED AND NEVER COME BACK.

THE CHANGE-OF-ADDRESS CARD WENT TO BOTH OLD AND NEW

As I mentioned, we're moving this summer. It's been so long since we moved, I've forgotten how many people and places need to know that we're not going to be at Van Altena Avenue anymore. The old days of simply leaving a change-of-address card with the post office are gone. Oh, the people and businesses that need us to go online to update them! At least we're moving to Main Street, which is a much simpler address than our old home on Van Altena Avenue.

If you moved as a geographical cure, would you tell your problem neighbors where you're going? Of course not. They're going to ask, "Where are you going?" You'd like to say, "Well, we're not sure." Really? You're moving but you don't know where you're going? No one's going to buy that, and besides, in a small town like Cedar Grove, everyone knows exactly where you're going anyway.

But wouldn't it be great to say something like that to our sins? Just tell them, "We're moving!" If they ask where, just say, "Not sure, but we're not staying here." This is what Paul speaks of in Romans 6 when he describes the newness of life that comes with Baptism: "For one who has died has been set free from sin. . . .

For sin will have no dominion over you, since you are not under law but under grace" (vv. 7, 14). In Galatians, Paul celebrates this freedom, saying simply, "For freedom Christ has set us free; stand firm therefore, and do not submit again to a yoke of slavery" (5:1). This is a wonderful promise of freedom from the controlling power of sin. We have moved through Baptism, not merely from one address to another but through death to a new resurrection in the sight of God.

Years ago, when I was restoring our 1917 Ford Model T car, it wasn't running quite right one day. After a couple of frustrating hours working on it, I came in for lunch. To console myself, I told Holly and the kids that at least in heaven the Model T would run right. Our seven-year-old daughter, Christy, right away said, "No, Dad, Model T's don't go to heaven." I was a little sad to hear this and so I asked her why Model T's don't go to heaven. She said, with that tone seven-year-olds use when they have to explain the world to adults, "Model T's don't go to heaven because Model T's never die." Well, all right then, that sounds good to me.

Some things stay here. The resurrection won't move everything. Even deserving Model T Fords might not go to heaven. Overall, this is good news. We're moving, but not everything about this world is coming with us. When God takes us to heaven, there's room only for us but not our sins and their penalty. It is often said that you don't see a U-Haul truck following a hearse to the gravesite. True—we go empty-handed into the tomb. But not only do we go empty into the grave; all the more, we come through the resurrection free of the past. There is no waiting U-Haul truck packed with our sins, no Two Men and a Truck crew loading up printed records of all we've done. When God takes us to heaven, He takes us alone.

Paul describes the brilliance of the change from this life to the life of heaven when Jesus returns: "Behold! I tell you a mystery. We shall not all sleep, but we shall all be changed, in a moment, in the twinkling of an eye, at the last trumpet. For the trumpet will sound, and the dead will be raised imperishable, and we shall be changed. For this perishable body must put on the imperishable, and this mortal body must put on immortality" (1 Corinthians 15:51–53). In the resurrection, all of the past is left as dust beneath our feet. Any protests against us, any record of our wrongs, they're lost in shouts of amazed victory. Paul captures this in the next verses: "O Death, where is your victory? O Death, where is your sting?" (v. 55). In the resurrection, we'll have made the ultimate move. Death and sin are not coming with us. We're forgiven, and nothing will demonstrate that more than our resurrection into heaven's victory. We're forgiven, and in the resurrection, we'll be moving far, far away.

But in This Town, Everyone Knows

Like I said, we're moving from our quiet street, Van Altena Avenue, which dead-ends a block west of us. We're going to South Main Street, which is the main road north and south through town. We're going to be easier to find than ever, and that's fine with us. It would be sad if our friends never came over because they couldn't find us. But no one can get lost on Main Street in Cedar Grove.

However, if you're moving for the geographical cure, don't you wish you could move somewhere that's completely off the GPS grid? Move and leave it all behind. When a place has turned sour and your heart sinks every time you pull into the driveway, you want to leave and never be found again.

Unfortunately, our sins have planted a tracking device in each of us. This began early in the biblical record. God warned Cain, "If you do not do well, sin is crouching at the door" (Genesis 4:7). David knew the nearness of his sin as he wrote, "For I know my transgressions, and my sin is ever before me" (Psalm 51:3). The sin that we wish to scrub out of our lives still clings to us. It comes with us to every new home, every new office, every new vacation rental. It leaps out of the moving truck before the back door is opened. It's settled into the house while we're still carrying in the couch. Despite our best intentions, many of our same failings will be repeated. Paul summed this up for us: "For I do not understand my own actions. For I do not do what I want, but I do the very thing I hate. . . . For I do not do the good I want, but the evil I do not want is what I keep on doing" (Romans 7:15, 19).

So, while we look forward to the complete freedom of our resurrection move, we still have the presence of sin here. We can't outrun it, move up beyond it, or uninvite it. We have faith in God's promise of our resurrection and the eventual freedom from sin. But we can't move to that heavenly home yet. Today, we're still living where sin crouches at the door. We need forgiveness as the answer that moves our guilt far away.

Pack It All Up—You Won't Be Coming Back

When you move, you don't plan to return. We have really enjoyed our twenty-three years at our home on Van Altena Avenue, but we don't plan on coming back. We won't be asking the new owners for a special return price five years from now. Moving is a one-way experience.

Forgiveness is a one-way trip. Forgiveness packs up our sin and its guilt and sends it away with no chance of a return. God's version of the geographical cure works better than we would have ever expected. This is a clean-sweep move with no return address given. It is like my friend Brady Ingles, who runs a motorcycle restoration business. People send him bikes from all around the country to restore but also simply to tune up. One man trucks his 1970s Hondas from Texas to Wisconsin just for a tune-up! That's going a long way to fix a small problem, but that's the reputation Brady has. Trucking from Texas for a tune-up makes sense if the problems

FORGIVENESS IS A ONE-WAY TRIP.

will all stay in Wisconsin. When that Honda goes back to Texas, it's perfect. The broken pieces all stay here with Brady.

The Bible shows this same principle with the scapegoat as described in Leviticus 16. The scapegoat was the second of two goats chosen for a sin offering. One goat was killed as a sacrifice, and the blood of the goat along with the blood of a bull was sprinkled over the altar to cleanse Israel from their sin. Then the second goat was brought to Moses' brother, Aaron:

> And Aaron shall lay both his hands on the head of the live goat, and confess over it all the iniquities of the people of Israel, and all their transgressions, all their sins. And he shall put them on the head of the goat and send it away into the wilderness by the hand of a man who is in readiness. The goat shall bear all their iniquities on itself to a remote area, and he shall let the goat go free in the wilderness. (vv. 21–22)

Here is what we have always wished could be done with our sins and their guilt: let them be put on another and driven out of our home. What a geographical cure! We remain in our home while that which torments us is driven away. This sending away of our sins and guilt at first sounds like our initial image of cleansing. Cleansing was like the blood of the first goat in Leviticus 16, when Aaron sprinkled the blood seven times: "And he shall sprinkle some of the blood on it with his finger seven times, and cleanse it and consecrate it from the uncleannesses of the people of Israel" (v. 19). But with cleansing comes the question, where did the stain go? We're glad to see the sparkling newness of something just cleaned. But if we don't know where the stain went, perhaps we worry that it'll return.

However, with the scapegoat, we have the perfect combination of opposites. We have the hidden and the revealed. We know exactly where something is, but we haven't got a clue how to find it. We know exactly where our sins have gone, but we can never find them again. If we were in that camp, watching the priest, we would have the certainty that our sins have been placed on the goat.

> **WE KNOW EXACTLY WHERE OUR SINS HAVE GONE, BUT WE CAN NEVER FIND THEM AGAIN.**

But then the goat is driven away from the camp. The man who leads it out comes back but the goat does not. Good. The goat and our sins are gone. Let's sleep well. But then, imagine waking up the next morning. What's the last thing you want to see? The goat! Wouldn't that goat standing by your tent, chewing on your ropes, be your worst nightmare? In that horrible dream, the goat not only comes back, but he chooses your tent for a snack. You should have moved.

The good news, of course, is that the goat isn't going to come back. The wilderness was a harsh world. The goat had no chance against the predators that were waiting there. The goat wouldn't make it through the day, and he certainly wasn't going to come back from the dead. Carrying our sins, he's on a one-way trip.

YOU CAN ONLY DO THIS WITH A GOAT

The scapegoat is a wonderful solution as long as it involves a goat. But at least two aspects of the atonement by the scapegoat leave us with serious questions. As attractive as the sending of sins away is, can it really be so?

First, the goat is innocent, and yet the sins of all the people are put upon him. Is that just? Can injustice ever bring justice? Can innocence carry the sins of others? If you accuse an innocent man of what he's never done, he'll protest. If you insist he carry the sins that he didn't do, it all seems wrong. Can this sort of wrong ever be right?

Even if we can imagine sins being transferred to someone else, there's the problem of leaving the goat behind. Let the goat carry the sins of the camp, but then imagine the goat getting to ask a few questions. The man is about to leave the goat in the wilderness. The goat would have to ask, "You're leaving? You're leaving me here? But it's getting dark. I don't know my way back. I don't like the looks of this place." I doubt that the man would have an answer. The goat has already done the impossible work of bearing the sins of the people and carrying

> **BUT NOW THE IMPOSSIBLE HAS TURNED CRUEL.**

them out of the camp. But now the impossible has turned cruel. The innocent goat is left to die, alone, outside the camp, with a burden that we can't imagine.

If the goat were more than a goat, this would never happen. If the goat had even the simplest understanding of what was going to happen, he wouldn't move. If the weight of sin wasn't overwhelming, then the certainty of death would certainly paralyze him. His options would be simple: Don't move. Stay in the camp. Argue for justice. What's the worst that can be done to you? Death? That's exactly what's coming anyway. No, the scapegoat will only work with a clueless goat who somehow trusts the one who leads him to his death.

ON THE OTHER HAND, IT COULD WORK WITH GOD

The scapegoat method will work with an ignorant goat. Or it will work with God. If you're the scapegoat, you either know nothing, or you have to know everything. You either can't see what's coming in the next hour, or you've planned this for eternity. The scapegoat solution will only work with the extremes, a goat or God.

Let's go through our two objections to the scapegoat approach again—not with a goat but with the Son of God as that sacrifice. Our first objection was that the Innocent One is bearing the sins of all. Can you make the innocent guilty? Can His guilt, given by God, be actual guilt that empties our accounts? Only God can make this judgment. To our minds, it seems both terribly unjust and impossible. He did no wrong, and yet we cast our sins entirely upon Him, making Him to be sin. That transformation is exactly what Paul describes: "For our sake He made Him to be sin who knew no sin, so that in Him we might become the righteousness of God" (2 Corinthians 5:21). That bearing of sin couldn't be done in the abstract of a heavenly court. It had to be done in the flesh, as Paul notes: "For God has done what the law, weakened by the flesh, could not do. By sending His own Son in the likeness of sinful flesh and for sin, He condemned sin in the flesh" (Romans 8:3). That condemnation was focused on the flesh He bore on the cross. "Christ redeemed us from the curse of the law by becoming a curse for us—for it is written, 'Cursed is everyone who is hanged on a tree'" (Galatians 3:13).

How can this be, the innocent Son of God being burdened with the guilt of the world? Our objection with the goat was that it was both innocent and only a goat. Now the pendulum of wonder has swung completely to the other side. Here is the utterly innocent God, the Giver of the Law Himself. Furthermore, He is the Creator of all things and under no compulsion whatever to make this incredible exchange of innocence for guilt. But perhaps that is the answer. If the goat is seemingly too insignificant to be the bearer of all the sins, then let the measure of worth go to the far extreme. If a nameless goat is too little, then let the only-begotten Son take its place. Let all the sins of the world be drawn into the utter vacuum of His perfection. If He will open Himself to that judgment, then no sin can remain here, clinging to us. No, His perfection will draw all the guilt to Himself.

But if we put this enormous burden onto Him, how can He function? Maybe the answer is a bit like emptying our house for the move. Today is Friday, the day that the recycling truck comes through town. Now that we're moving, our recycling bin and garbage container are maxed out. Our containers are so heavy that

I've told Holly that when the truck picks up one of them, it might tip the truck over onto its side. So far it hasn't happened, but we really loaded them up this week, so we'll see.

If simply moving our stuff a mile brings out that much weight, what is the weight of the sins of the world? What is the cubic concentration of all the guilt the world has ever felt? How debilitating is that load? How can the Son of God move under such a load?

For that, we have the scene of Jesus praying in the Garden of Gethsemane on Maundy Thursday night. Here we can see Him settling under this load. Imagine those hours of prayer as the weight lifter taking on a bar-bending load that has crushed every other man. We stand in awe, joining the disciples in prayer that this load can be lifted and the journey beneath it started. Who can grasp the burden that He was about to carry? As Jesus contemplated this final burden in the coming hours, no wonder He asked if it could be avoided. But with courage and love, this strong man settled Himself under the bar and lifted the burden. Silently He bore the injustice with all His innocent strength. He walked beneath this load to His death. He knew that on the cross, the load would only increase as He was forsaken by the Father, the only one who truly understood what He was enduring. He also knew that only death on the cross would lift the load from His shoulders. Then, with triumph, at the end of those six hours, He cast away the bar with its weight of guilt. The journey was done. Hear Him say, "It is finished" (John 19:30).

> SILENTLY HE BORE THE INJUSTICE WITH ALL HIS INNOCENT STRENGTH.

What a contrast He is in this walk to what we expect of the scapegoat. If the goat knew what was coming, it would refuse to move from the camp. But Christ knows exactly what's coming, and He walks toward it. He knows that when that load of guilt is fully settled upon Him, He must carry it out of the camp. Hebrews 13 sums it up: "So Jesus also suffered outside the gate in order to sanctify the people through His own blood" (v. 12).

That leads us to the final question. The goat, if it knew its fate, would never trust the man who was leading it. It would never stay behind when the man left it, though the goat was likely tethered in place for that very reason. Surely the goat, if it had any sense of danger, would bolt back to the camp, wouldn't it?

Not only does Christ accept this fate, but it's His own desire. This isn't a divided divinity, Father set against His Son. No. Father, Son, and Spirit, one indivisible God, together have always had this plan. We have been chosen as His own from "before the foundation of the world" (Ephesians 1:4). Jesus makes this clear when He describes Himself as the Shepherd: "For this reason the Father loves Me, because I lay down My life that I may take it up again. No one takes it from Me, but I lay it down of My own accord. I have authority to lay it down, and I have authority to take it up again" (John 10:17–18). He's not a goat marched off to an unjust death. He's the Shepherd who saves His flock by His eternal choice to die. By His single death, He destroys death. His choice to die for others compounds His choice. He chooses to die, and therefore He chooses also to rise from the dead.

The scapegoat can only take our sins away. That in itself is wonderful. But what if you loved the goat? The day it was led away was terribly sad for you, as you knew it would never return. But what a joy we have with the One who carries all the world's sins. Good Friday is not the end. Yes, He carries the sins outside of the city and bears them alone. But He's not lost to us. He returns on Easter. His return is not the frightening return of the scapegoat, somehow alive, and still carrying the sins with him. No, Easter brings us the Shepherd who has risen of His own power. He who bore the guilt of world and endured the agony of hell brings back

HE WHO CARRIED OFF OUR SINS BRINGS ONLY PEACE IN HIS RETURN.

no hint of that guilt or penalty. Instead, His opening words to the disciples are "Peace be with you" (John 20:19). He who carried off our sins brings only peace in His return.

LOST IN THE EASTERN MIST

We live on the western shore of Lake Michigan. Our little town of Cedar Grove is about a mile and a half from the shore. Stand at the end of the sidewalk in front of our new home and you have a clear view all the way to the lake. I like living on the western shore since we're often in the clear while clouds and fog build up over the lake. The lake varies from eighty to a hundred miles wide, and so our eastern horizon is the endless blue water. If clouds build up over the lake, we're usually in the clear. Let the lake-effect snow get driven by the northwest wind. It's all going to Michigan, not us. For them, that western wind brings clouds and snow while we stand in the sunshine.

Isn't this the wonderful truth of our forgiveness? We stand safely on this far shore while our sins have been carried far beyond us. To the east, on a hill far out of sight, our sins were lifted by the one Man who could carry such a load. That's where our sins remain, as far from us in space and time as we can imagine. Psalm 103 describes this blessed distance: "For as high as the heavens are above the earth, so great is His steadfast love toward those who fear Him; as far as the east is from the west, so far does He remove our transgressions from us" (vv. 11–12).

Here is a wonderful separation. We live on the far western shore and God has made a barrier between ourselves and our sins. Our sins have been carried away and cast out of our sight. We're the people destined for a distant shore. One day, God will raise us to the eternity of heaven with Him. Even now, our sins are already far beyond us, carried away by the Savior.

We can't see the distant hill of Calvary where our sins have gone. Because of this, perhaps we might fear that what is hidden to us is still in the sight of God. Should we worry that God can still see our sins and is waiting to return them to us? In Isaiah, Hezekiah describes what God has done with our sins: "In love You have delivered my life from the pit of destruction, for You have cast all my sins behind Your back" (Isaiah 38:17). God has chosen to place our sins upon His Son. But when that burden was carried and the penalty paid, God put that behind Him. What an answer this is when we bring up our sins and the penalty that we fear is still waiting for us. God can say, "I am done with all that. That black day has passed. I have put it behind My back, and with it, your sins are forgotten." If that seems better than we can believe, here is the promise of God Himself: "I, I am He who blots out your transgressions for My own sake, and I will not remember your sins" (Isaiah 43:25). God has chosen to place our sins out of His sight and mind. They are not reserved for another day, waiting to threaten us. No, they are completely sent away.

This distance from our sins creates a wonderful vacuum. It's like moving your home. We've got most everything packed away now, including our bedroom mirror and the living room clock. We know they're in boxes, but we still glance over to where they've been for twenty-three years. They're gone, but we keep looking.

Perhaps we do this still with our sins, even though they're forgiven and moved far out of sight. Perhaps you still look for those sins where they've always been. Do you still check your appearance with sin's cracked mirror? Do you still time today with the clock of your past? God has put away the record of your sins. The mirror you dreaded is boxed up. God's complete forgiveness has taken the past away. By Christ's work on that distant cross, our sins have been forgiven and moved so far away that they will never be seen again.

DO YOU STILL CHECK YOUR APPEARANCE WITH SIN'S CRACKED MIRROR?

With God, the geographical cure actually works. While I can't guarantee that moving will solve the challenges with your neighbors, the schools, or your children's friends, moving works with God. God has geographically cured us of our sins. He has loaded them onto the only One who could possibly carry such a load. The innocent Son has stepped under that crushing load, grasped the bar with His callused hands, and lifted the weight. He took every single sin to the far shore of Calvary on that dark day. When it was done, He cast down the load and gave up His life. But as He was buried, so was our sin. He has risen, but our sins stay buried. Take heart; your sins are far, far away. No mere scapegoat, but the greatest of all time, God Himself, has carried them over the horizon. Their guilt and penalty will never return. Our sins have been taken far, far away.

BUTTERNUT—THE WOOD THAT'S FAR AWAY

Butternut is the one wood we're using that might not be common to most woodworkers. But I have a very good reason for its inclusion. First, a bit of description is in order. Butternut is a relative of the better-known black walnut. Like the walnut, it's valued for the nuts it produces. But it is a beautiful wood in itself with a tan color that's lighter than black walnut. Butternut is relatively soft and straight grained. It is a favorite wood for carvers, and it's often been used for church altars and lecterns.

Besides the beauty of butternut, there's another reason for its use on our cube of forgiveness. As you may know, Holly and I lived in Butternut, Wisconsin, for the twelve years that I served as pastor of St. Paul's Lutheran Church there. How did our little town get its name? The story I often heard was that Butternut was the farthest north that the butternut tree could be found growing along the Soo railroad line that went through town. So the butternut tree, growing in Butternut, Wisconsin, is the wood far away, found at the very end of the line.

What a perfect wood when we think of our forgiveness, which is far away. At the very end of the line, on an altar of the hard, rough wood of the cross, our forgiveness was placed. Not with the carver's delicate touch, but with the rough pounding of the nails was forgiveness shaped. Let's imagine the cross being the butternut of God's forest, the last tree, the one farthest away. There at the end of the line stands the tree that keeps our sins far, far away from us.

BLUE—THE KINGDOM IS COMING

Blue is the perfect color as we focus on what is far away. Blue is the color of heaven, drawing our eyes and mind upward. It's the color that reminds us to fix our eyes on Jesus, who went into the heavens and from the heavens will return. Blue in Advent reminds us to prepare for His eventual return. Blue is the color our minds might fix upon as we consider that our citizenship is in heaven, and from there, Jesus will come to transform us.

So, let blue bring us the promises of heaven. That will be our ultimate move. We won't need to pack for heaven since we're already being transformed for it. Our sins have been already packed, loaded, and carried off. Now we're no longer tied to that dark horizon; we've already crossed to the safe shore. Our sins have been taken far away, and in time, we'll be taken far, far away into the heaven God has prepared for us.

HYMNS OF FORGIVENESS

The scapegoat took the sins outside the camp, and Jesus did this in the final sense. The hymn "I Lay My Sins on Jesus" expresses this burden of sin being placed on Jesus and His willingness to carry all these sins far from us:

I lay my sins on Jesus,
  The spotless Lamb of God;
He bears them all and frees us
  From the accursed load.
I bring my guilt to Jesus
  To wash my crimson stains
Clean in His blood most precious
  Till not a spot remains.

I lay my wants on Jesus;
  All fullness dwells in Him;
He heals all my diseases;
  My soul He does redeem.
I lay my griefs on Jesus,
  My burdens and my cares;
He from them all releases;
  He all my sorrows shares. (*LSB* 606:1–2)

When our sins are carried away, we can rejoice. He has the answer for our sins, no matter how far they've gone. This wonderful news is in the Christmas hymn "Joy to the World":

No more let sins and sorrows grow
  Nor thorns infest the ground;
He comes to make His blessings flow
  Far as the curse is found,
Far as the curse is found,
  Far as, far as the curse is found.
  (*LSB* 387:3)

Though our sins have spread like thorns on cursed ground, His forgiveness has more than matched them. He has snatched up our sins wherever they're found and taken them on Himself as though they were His. Our sins are truly gone, for He has carried them far away.

DISCUSSION QUESTIONS

1. The theme of the chapter was moving. When have you moved? How much work was it? What was the reason for the move?

2. The attraction of the geographical cure is a fresh start with the security of physical distance between us and our problems. How is this a good definition of some key aspects of forgiveness?

3. The chapter discussed the ultimate geographical cure of the resurrection and our entry into heaven. See the descriptions of this in 1 Corinthians 15:50–55 and 1 Thessalonians 4:13–18. How will the change of the resurrection and our being lifted into heaven express the essence of God's forgiveness over all our sins?

4. We're moving to a different home on Main Street, and everybody in town knows it. But when have you moved or wanted to move and wished you could leave no forwarding address? How completely can a person move and be lost from his or her past?

5. While it might be hard to escape our past, how does the scapegoat image serve as a way in which distance and time separate us from our sins?

6. We noted that the scapegoat method presumes an innocent, unknowing goat. But how is the drama so much greater when the one carrying our sins is the completely innocent, all-knowing Son of God?

7. In our sidebars, the color blue and the distant and unusual butternut tree were the examples of forgiveness that takes our sins as far away as possible. How are these images of beauty and distance a good match for forgiveness?

Many

I need bigger speakers. I'm writing this on a beautiful August afternoon while sitting on the deck at our house on Van Altena Avenue. George Strait is singing through the speakers on my computer. On a perfect afternoon, with no wind and no traffic, those tiny speakers are just loud enough. We're moving in two weeks, and this afternoon is the perfect way to say goodbye to our deck and backyard.

But sometimes, it's not perfect back here. The deck looks over our backyard toward a vacant lot. The vacant lot faces Highway D, the main east-west road in our town. We're a half block from the edge of town at the bottom of a hill. The trucks pulling into town come down the hill and hit the town's twenty-five-miles-per-hour speed limit. I'm sure you can hear the exhaust brakes popping as the trucks slow down. On the other hand, the Harleys going west up the hill, out of town, are determined to make even more noise than the trucks. So, there's this battle going on between the trucks and the Harleys. George Strait doesn't have a chance of being heard.

I need bigger speakers. The little speakers on my computer can't compete against the trucks and bikes. Now, don't worry. I'm not seriously thinking of getting huge speakers. If I did, our kind neighbors would likely volunteer to help us move to our new house even sooner. But it does cross the mind. Big speakers, like the ones you had when you were in college, would be perfect. Remember those monsters? You put them in the dorm windows, facing out, and you entertained the whole campus. If I got big enough speakers, I wouldn't even know the trucks and bikes were going by.

That's the point of this facet of forgiveness. One sound over-whelming another is forgiveness. We have very selective hearing. We are acutely attuned to the words of condemnation that remind us of our sins. We can hear the whispered accusations from decades ago. We replay the harshest words that have been said to us and we make them even sharper than they were when they were new.

We need bigger speakers. We need a sound that can overwhelm those condemning words with the words of forgiveness. Our last two facets, here and in chapter 7, center on the contrast of Many and One. First, we'll hear the many, repeated words of God, who tirelessly announces our forgiveness. God provides us the bigger speakers and the sound that can drown out our guilt. However, He gives us more than just sound. With Him, we have His words, signifying the wealth of His sacrifice, which calm the furious guilt we so often hear. After we hear the crescendo of God's words in this facet, we'll turn to the last aspect. In the last, quiet facet, we'll hear an equally reassuring word. But the stress there will be on the soft, single sentence that brings forgiveness. God speaks not only in thundering tones but also in the still, small voice that silences everything else.

These last two facets will stress our hearing of forgiveness. This completes our use of several senses through the six facets. The first two, Clean and Covered, stressed sight, as the stain was either cleaned or covered with the life of Christ and the darkness of the tomb. The second pair, Fixed and Far, had a more tactile feel. The first, Fixed, used the reassuring feeling we have when something is in its place. Our hand reaches again and again for the calming feel that, yes, it's there. So, forgiveness is fixed with the strength of the nails that will never move. Then there was the clean sweep of the sins sent far away. The resurrection will finally take us away from the frailties of our lives when our bodies are raised. But already the scapegoat has taken the entire load of sin onto Himself. Our camp is empty, our sins left yesterday, and none of what we fear will ever come back.

Now, after seeing and feeling, it's time to hear forgiveness. We need to hear the forgiveness that fits so well with the nature of God as He speaks to the world. Jesus as the Word of God is the promise of forgiveness, as He reminds us in John 3:17: "For God did not send His Son into the world to condemn the world, but in order that the world might be saved through Him." It is the word that brings us life, as Jesus said in John 5:24: "Truly, truly, I say to you, whoever hears My word and believes Him who sent Me has eternal life." So, in this facet, we'll stress the abundance of God's Word and the relief it brings us by announcing forgiveness. When we know it's the message of forgiveness, we're glad to have His Word shouted out.

Along with the volume of His message, there is another aspect to this final pair of facets. It's not one of our five senses, but rather it's time. Besides the overwhelming sound of forgiveness, we have the endlessness of God's speaking. When God speaks forgiveness, He never stops. God holds the high note of forgiveness forever. While we remember the words that have condemned us, God can outlast even our memories. His words endlessly tell of the sacrifice of Jesus and the

> **GOD HOLDS THE HIGH NOTE OF FORGIVENESS FOREVER.**

boundless love that sent Him to the cross. Our enemies will perish and their words will be finally silenced. But the words of God are without end, as Jesus said: "Heaven and earth will pass away, but My words will not pass away" (Luke 21:33). We'll be with Him forever because His words of forgiveness will never end.

NOT EVERYONE LISTENS

Let's go back to my earlier image of trying to listen to music with the trucks and bikes going back and forth. I understand that the truckers are doing their job, slowing down as they come into town. I'm glad they're not blowing into town at sixty miles per hour, so let them hit those exhaust brakes if they have to. After all, they're working here.

But excess noise gets a bit more annoying when you're at a concert and other people are as noisy as a semi pulling into town. These are the people who sit right in front of you and never stop talking. Never, not once. They're telling endless stories so loud that you hear them as much as any music. Did they listen to the concert? Not one song. They never heard a word. And because of them, you didn't either. The music was there, but with those people beside you, you hardly heard a note.

Those are the speakers we hear so often. You don't need to go to a concert to hear these voices. You and I bring the voices ourselves and put them on an endlessly repeating loop. Through the speakers of our memory, we hear the entire chorus of voices past. Unfortunately, we usually tune in to the voices of anger and disappointment, accusation and abandonment. These are the voices that want to pull us away from God. Paul lists those things that try to tear us from God: "Who shall separate us from the love of Christ? Shall tribulation, or distress, or persecution, or famine, or nakedness, or danger, or sword?" (Romans 8:35). We hear the voices that recount and expand on our wrongs, and like a vintage vinyl record, we have not only the words but all the pops and scratches that came with those words. We prompt those recordings by saying, to ourselves and others, "I remember when she said . . ." *Remember* is hardly the word. To remember suggests that we have packed it away but can find it if we need to. No, we have not packed these words away, buried somewhere like the box of old vinyl records that I have taped shut down in the basement. No, the voices that accuse us gather no dust and never hide in an unmarked

THE VOICES THAT ACCUSE US GATHER NO DUST AND NEVER HIDE IN AN UNMARKED BOX.

box. Just like the music that keeps playing even when we've taken off our headphones, so our memories play the voices even when we've tried to shut them off.

I'm afraid of hearing even one of these memory voices. If I tune in to one of them, seriously slowing down my life to acknowledge that what it says is right, what will that say to all the other memories? Won't that bring them all on? It's like asking a class, "Any questions?" Unless you do that with your hand on the door and the class already five minutes overtime, be prepared. There could be questions. And if you hear one, you need to hear the next and the next and the next . . . Listen to the first accusation and you're open to all the others. No wonder we try to avoid the voices and perhaps even deny there's anything wrong at all.

If only denial worked. If only we could find the mute button on our conscience. If only we could find a perfect silence in which to escape. However, we can't escape the sad truth. We are sinners and that reality can't be silenced. If we try, the sounds of our sin still echo within us. David knew about this when he described the effect of his denial of sin: "For when I kept silent, my bones wasted away through my groaning all day long" (Psalm 32:3). There is no silence within me. The accusations of my sin are a vibration that wears away at the structure of my life. Like a subwoofer that is more felt than heard, so guilt speaks deeply within each of us. It becomes the rhythm section of our life with an endless beat.

I Need Bigger Speakers and a Better Speaker Salesman

When I was in college, I bought new speakers for my Pioneer amplifier of which I was very proud. I went to the local stereo store and the salesman was happy to help. He showed me these two beautiful speakers, each one almost three feet tall. This being the mid-1970s, he put on the group Boston and their song "More Than a Feeling." He cranked up the amp and stood back. What sound! I was sold before Boston got to the second verse. (By the way, Boston is playing that song through my computer now. Sadly, it doesn't sound anything like those old speakers.)

I had those speakers throughout college and graduate school. I was the guy who put the speakers in his dorm window and shared the music with the rest of campus. Those speakers were not some little, easy-listening bookshelf pieces. They were made to blow out the windows and catch you on the sidewalk across the street. When they played a song, you heard it.

Forgiveness needs those speakers. Forgiveness needs to drown out the many voices that have accumulated in a chorus against us. Forgiveness needs to fill our rooms and explode past our windows. Forgiveness wants to be the music that is shared across the street. Forgiveness is a sound so powerful, it makes our enemies into frustrated mimes who cannot get beyond their imaginary boxes. Their lips may be moving, but their accusations are never heard. Forgiveness is the sound that reverberates through our lives. Forgiveness brings big speakers.

> **FORGIVENESS IS A SOUND SO POWERFUL, IT MAKES OUR ENEMIES INTO FRUSTRATED MIMES WHO CANNOT GET BEYOND THEIR IMAGINARY BOXES.**

BRING ON THE DUEL

Imagine a high school basketball game where both schools bring their bands. The bands are seated on opposite sides of the gym. They don't play at the same time but alternate back and forth before the game and at halftime. The fans are not here for a flute and piccolo duet. They want sheer volume. So, let the other band play first. Let them stand up, lift those trumpets and trombones, and work the drummers all they want. But when they're done, it's time for our band to play. Pause for just a moment for effect and then let fly. They had five trumpets; we have fifteen. They had four trombones; we have sixteen. They had a snare drum and one bass drum. We have nine snare drummers, a perfectly synchronized line. And our five bass drummers never miss a beat. Contest? Battle of the bands? Not even close. We used that other band just to set the stage. We let them make a target of themselves, but from our first note, our band won.

That's the victory of forgiveness when volume matters. Listen to the way Paul describes the sounds of accusation and then the greater sound of forgiveness. Paul notes that the sin of Adam caused the death of all, but that the work of Christ exceeded that for all. "For if many died through one man's trespass, much more have the grace of God and the free gift by the grace of that one man Jesus Christ abounded for many. . . . For if, because of one man's trespass, death reigned through that one man, much more will those who receive the abundance of grace and the free gift of righteousness reign in life through the one man Jesus Christ" (Romans 5:15, 17). The sound of sin has echoed through all our lives from Adam on. But the greater sound of forgiveness has answered that ominous chord of sin. The triumphant tone of forgiveness has obliterated the words of condemnation. The louder the sound of sin, the greater the music of forgiveness grows. "Where sin increased, grace abounded all the more, so that, as sin reigned in death, grace also might reign through righteousness leading to eternal life through Jesus Christ our Lord" (Romans 5:20–21). In the battle of sin versus grace, let sin play every instrument it has. That only prompts grace to play all the louder. Sin is reduced to a futile flute trying to outdo a trumpet trio.

THAT'S THE VOLUME. WHAT ARE THE WORDS?

We know that the words of grace will outdo the accusations of our sins. The opening of this contest already shows that God will win in sheer volume. But we want more than just sound. We've heard the opening measures—but now listen. Here come the words.

That's the beauty of God's ongoing words on our behalf. He defeats the accusations of sin not only by the power of sound but by the meaning of His words. In Romans 8, Paul gives us that contrast between that which would condemn and the One who speaks on our behalf: "Who shall bring any charge against God's elect? It is God who justifies. Who is to condemn? Christ Jesus is the one who died—more than that, who was raised—who is at the right hand of God, who indeed is interceding for us" (vv. 33–34). Paul holds up the audacity of anyone even trying to accuse those who are already justified by God. If God has already declared us to be just, who would ever try to accuse us? We've passed through the judgment of God by His grace. Who could possibly have a greater standard of holiness than God? Who could claim any higher understanding of the Commandments than the One who gave those Commandments? As Jesus said, "So if the Son sets you free, you will be free indeed" (John 8:36).

God has spoken the clearest words of forgiveness: "There is therefore now no condemnation for those who are in Christ Jesus" (Romans 8:1). Consider this the verdict announced in the courtroom. "Not guilty," the Judge declares. To us, this is wonderful relief. But our opponents explode in anger. They shout that we can't possibly be innocent. We can't be set free. What sort of justice is this that says there will be no condemnation for the likes of us?

To that outburst the Judge pounds His gavel and demands that the court be silent. The enemies still murmur, whispering to one another with words we'd rather not hear. The judgment is in, but it hasn't produced the silent acceptance we might have expected. Something more is needed.

To that need, God brings forward His Son to speak. Romans describes Him as He gives testimony to His payment given for our forgiveness: "Christ Jesus is the one who died—more than that, who was raised—who is at the right hand of God, who indeed is interceding for us" (8:34). To whom will the Judge listen? To the murmuring protesters who reject His judgment, or to His Son who kept the Law in order to give us His righteousness in exchange for our sin? The Judge will listen only to His Son.

What does the Son say in the heavenly courts on our behalf? We can only imagine. The intercession for us is indeed beyond our hearing and understanding, as Paul describes the work of the Holy Spirit also in Romans 8: "The Spirit Himself intercedes for us with groanings too deep for words. And He who searches hearts knows what is the mind of the Spirit, because the Spirit intercedes for the saints according to the will of God" (vv. 26–27). Perhaps the clearest words said for us by the Spirit and the Son might be a variation on the words Jesus said at the cross: "Father, forgive them, for they know not what they do" (Luke 23:34). This is the message we can hear over and over. Let His words of forgiveness be those you repeat. Let His words be the first to reach your ears. Make these words of forgiveness the soundtrack of your life, the endless loop of reassurance that you need. God declares no condemnation for us in Christ Jesus. Having been justified, we have peace with God. Nothing can separate us from the love of God. Hear those words over and over. They'll never be played too often.

That's the private music of forgiveness that we hear. In the soundtrack of forgiveness, we hear Jesus speak to us as He did to the woman caught in adultery: "'Where are they? Has no one condemned you?' She said, 'No one, Lord.' And Jesus said, 'Neither do I condemn you; go, and from now on sin no more'" (John 8:10–11). Imagine how often the woman repeated those words. "Neither do I condemn you." I suspect those words were every other memory for the rest of her life. When the whispers of her former life surrounded her, she had an answer. In her mind and in her heart, she heard only His words: "Neither do I condemn you; go, and from now on sin no more."

We need those words. This is the tune that should be stuck in our minds. This is the chorus we find ourselves repeating without even thinking of it. The echo of His words can become the rhythm of our daily walk. His words are the balance to the whispered condemnations we hear. But we drown them out by the repeated words that He's given us. Forgiveness is His song for the whole world, but forgiveness is also His song just for Himself and you. If you have yearned to find someone with whom you can share one special song, He has found you. The lyrics are already written in His words of forgiveness. Furthermore, He never tires of repeating those words, singing them with the same force and originality that they've always had. Forgiveness is the song He wrote for the world, the song He sings every day to you.

> **FORGIVENESS IS THE SONG HE WROTE FOR THE WORLD, THE SONG HE SINGS EVERY DAY TO YOU.**

IT'S ALL RIGHT—EVERYONE ELSE IS ALREADY SINGING

I enjoy music very much, but I can't sing. I have no natural rhythm. When people begin to clap their hands to a song, I smile and keep my hands in my pockets. If I try to clap in rhythm, people ask me what song I'm listening to.

But it wouldn't matter at a concert. Take me to a concert at a huge outdoor stadium. Crank up the speakers on stage and let the band start to play the one song we all came to hear. People are going to be singing because everyone knows the words. Even if we all sing, we won't drown out the band. If we make too much noise, they'll just turn up those speakers. So, sing away, or do whatever passes for singing if you're like me. That song will sound better than it ever did before. It might lack some subtle nuance that comes through on the studio recording. But nothing will match the excitement of singing with the crowd.

The words of forgiveness are meant to be multiplied by our singing with the crowd. The many words of Jesus spoken on our behalf are endlessly spoken by Him for our defense. But they're also repeated and multiplied by all those who hear and believe those words. Worship brings us together into the concert crowd where the melody of forgiveness sweeps us all along.

> **WORSHIP BRINGS US TOGETHER INTO THE CONCERT CROWD WHERE THE MELODY OF FORGIVENESS SWEEPS US ALL ALONG.**

Consider what an opportunity we have when we worship with those who share this forgiveness. We come together to give thanks for the forgiveness that allows us to be with Him and with each other. Forgiveness creates these relationships of grace. By that forgiveness, we all have equal access to His presence and mercy. There are no bad seats or pillars to block us. There's no last row where we can hear only an echo of what was sung. No, in worship, we're all gathered with the same Father who hears the one Son, announcing there is no condemnation for those who are in Christ Jesus.

In worship, we share the assurance of forgiveness. Look around in worship at your church and its people. Then, look beyond the walls that surround you and imagine all those across the world who are worshiping with you this same morning. Imagine all the lives cleansed by forgiveness. Look for—but never see—the sins that are covered in the deep darkness of the cross of Christ. Reassure yourself with another touch that the nails of the cross still hold your sins fast. There your sins are fixed. But then remind yourself that those sins are far, far away. They've been taken out of sight and beyond us entirely. They are east if we are west, north if we are south, high on a mountain if we are in the safe valley. No matter where God's people worship, our sins are far away with Him who was willing to carry them.

That is our certainty over His forgiveness. Our worship reminds us of these many images of forgiveness. When you sing a hymn, think of these images we've used and bring them onto the people surrounding you. In this place, sins are cleaned. Look there, the woman with her head bowed down. Her sins are covered. One pew ahead, that man knows the reassurance that his sins are fixed on the cross, but the woman next to him, oh, she needs the reassurance that her sins are far away. What a prayer to have while we sit during the offering. Maybe as we worship, we can pray for those around us who need this reassurance of forgiveness. Pray that they hear exactly the comfort they need. Even while you're praying for others, perhaps they're doing the same for you. Perhaps someone is praying right now that you'll have the particular image of forgiveness and the reassurance that you most need in the coming week. When we pray together, what a shared chorus we've taken up, singing with the crowd in the concert of the Son's forgiveness.

DARE TO BE ON THE STAGE

I enjoy asking my students this question: "If you could be onstage singing backup for a famous singer, who would that be?" What a great range of answers they have. Some are singers and groups I've heard of, but others have names that leave me asking, "Really? There's a group with that name?" Maybe I need to start listening to more than George Strait. Regardless of who they choose, the question is a happy thought. Wouldn't it be great to be at a concert and, right before the best song of the night, the band stops and the lead singer looks you in the eye and says, "Come up here. We can't do this song without you. Here's your mic. You know the words."

We can't do this song without you. You know the words. That's the wonderful truth of forgiveness. The words of forgiveness need not only big speakers. They need more speakers, and you're one of the many who are needed. Just as we silently pray for the words of forgiveness to be multiplied to those worshiping with us, so there's also a time for us to say those words ourselves. We aren't the lead singer. Jesus takes that role. We aren't going to invent the

WE CAN'T DO THIS SONG WITHOUT YOU. YOU KNOW THE WORDS.

words of forgiveness. That song was written long before us. We won't be singing these words alone. We're the backup singers and there's more than one of us. But there are times for us to take that microphone, look at least one person in the eye, and start singing the song of forgiveness.

Why sing backup when our small voices will never match His? Why have us clutter the stage of His performance? Why would anyone spend a second listening to us? It's true that God needs no one to improve His words. He isn't short on volume if He chooses. Our tiny voices would be as nothing to the One whose sound can split rocks, as in 1 Kings 19. Remember how God came to Elijah after his forty days of despair? God told Elijah to stand on the mountain and He would pass by. "And behold, the LORD passed by, and a great and strong wind tore the mountains and broke in pieces the rocks before the LORD, but the LORD was not in the wind. And after the wind an earthquake, but the LORD was not in the earthquake. And after the earthquake a fire, but the LORD was not in the fire. And after the fire the sound of a low whisper" (vv. 11–12). The true presence of God didn't come with the greatness and sheer volume that we expected. To the discouraged Elijah, overwhelming volume wasn't needed. Rather, God whispered to a man who had lost heart.

God doesn't need bigger speakers from us. But He can use the many words you and I can say. There are so many Elijahs in our lives, people who have lost hope. Our small voices may be exactly the sound of forgiveness they need. God uses a gentle surround sound with the song of forgiveness. He doesn't use a deafening frontal assault on those who need this message. He surrounds them with the repeated words of forgiveness that we share. Be one of the voices God uses and whisper that word into their ears. You might not be the first to say those words of forgiveness, but for that moment,

GOD USES A GENTLE SURROUND SOUND WITH THE SONG OF FORGIVENESS.

you may be the only one saying them. They'll come again from others, but this is your moment. You are the speaker, the one who multiplies the many words of forgiveness and gives them in perfect timing.

I Still Need Bigger Speakers

We're in our new house now and it's a beautiful late afternoon. I'm in the backyard writing and our new neighbor is mowing her lawn next door. It's not nearly as loud as the trucks and the bikes we used to hear, but even her Toro is louder than my little computer speakers. Maybe that's the point. No matter where we are, bigger speakers are needed. Forgiveness needs bigger speakers. The noise of our world will always try to drown out the song of God's forgiveness. Even if the noise of the world comes from inside ourselves, we need God's words of forgiveness to be amplified until they're all we can hear. We can hear the words of forgiveness from the many who worship with us. We can be the speakers ourselves as we prayerfully send those words on to others. We even get to take the stage and say the words ourselves. Someone close to you needs to hear the song of forgiveness. Be the speaker that His forgiveness has made you.

NORTHERN RED OAK—TOO MANY PIECES TO COUNT

Red oak is the king of cabinet woods, at least in the Northeast and North Central states. This sturdy, beautiful wood grows over the eastern half of the United States and Canada and is the most common hardwood sold. Strong, stable, and beautiful, it has every positive trait. Its bold grain is distinctive and takes a wide range of stain. Red oak makes outstanding furniture, cabinets, and floors.

Our university chapel floor is made of red oak. The floor is almost sixty years old and still looks beautiful. The floor is a pattern of alternating blocks, each block holding five pieces of wood. The five pieces in each block alternate direction, one block arranged horizontally and the next block vertically. Within a 2-foot square, there are 125 small pieces of oak veneer plywood. Our chapel's wood floor is 108 feet by 97 feet, and so, with 10,476 square feet, we have approximately 327,375 pieces of oak making up the chapel floor. The alternating arrangement in direction and the natural differences in the grain and color make every square foot beautifully unique.

Walk into our chapel and, without thinking, you'll walk over hundreds of these pieces. Every block of five is beautiful and every one of them can hold you up. Rarely would you notice any one piece, but for decades they've supported everyone who has worshiped in our chapel.

Isn't this the beauty and strength of the many words of forgiveness? How many words of intercession have been said for you by Jesus? How many pleas for you have been murmured by the Spirit? They're beyond any counting, far more than even the oak of our chapel. How often have we stood upon those unheard words? Every day they've been our support, whether we've heard them or not. But the unending words of forgiveness make a solid floor for us and pave our approach to God. Arrange the pieces of oak on your cube to show off the variety of color and beautiful grain. On this parquet floor of forgiveness, rich in color, we come to stand in His grace.

GREEN—THE LONG SEASON OF GROWING

Green is the color of growing, the color of the long season of Trinity. Green is the color that lets us study all the words of Jesus and the farthest reaches of the lectionary's journey through the Old Testament and the Epistles. Green is the color we put on our altars in late spring when we're hoping to see the coming summer's growth in lawns and gardens. As grass and gardens flourish, we hope that our faith does the same through summer and fall.

Green is the perfect color for the many words of forgiveness. Picture the richness of the lawn of your dreams. Look at your neighbor's garden. What a kaleidoscope. It has every possible shade of green. Go for a drive through midsummer fields. Every different crop has a distinct shade. The many words of forgiveness lifted up for us are such a wide range of green. Each of the many words of forgiveness, repeated day after day for us, is always new and fresh. Forgiveness is never a tiresome repetition. Each time we hear the words, they're as satisfying as the freshest fruit from the garden. Let summer come and let green remind us that forgiveness is boundless and always new.

HYMNS OF FORGIVENESS

This chapter has used the songs we sing as the image of forgiveness. We can begin with our small voices, which God hears in mercy. A priceless example of this is the beloved hymn "What a Friend We Have in Jesus":

> Are we weak and heavy laden,
>   Cumbered with a load of care?
> Precious Savior, still our refuge—
>   Take it to the Lord in prayer.
> Do thy friends despise, forsake thee?
>   Take it to the Lord in prayer.
> In His arms He'll take and shield thee;
>   Thou wilt find a solace there.
>   (*LSB* 770:3)

"What a Friend We Have in Jesus" describes our small voice reaching God, but there are many hymns that picture a great choir, saints here and countless saints in heaven, singing praises for God's forgiveness. The beauty and majesty of heaven's choir and also Jesus' words spoken for us come together in another hymn, "Alleluia! Sing to Jesus":

Alleluia! Bread of heaven,
    Here on earth our food, our stay;

Alleluia! Here the sinful
    Flee to You from day to day.

Intercessor, Friend of sinners,
    Earth's Redeemer, hear our plea

Where the songs of all the sinless
    Sweep across the crystal sea. (*LSB* 821:3)

Given these images of heaven, we can only imagine the volume of our singing and the endlessness of the songs of heaven. A wonderful example is "What Wondrous Love Is This":

To God and to the Lamb I will sing,
    I will sing;

To God and to the Lamb I will sing;

To God and to the Lamb,
    Who is the great I AM,

While millions join the theme, I will sing,
    I will sing,

While millions join the theme, I will sing.

And when from death I'm free, I'll sing on,
    I'll sing on;

And when from death I'm free, I'll sing on.

And when from death I'm free,
    I'll sing His love for me,

And through eternity I'll sing on,
    I'll sing on,

And through eternity I'll sing on.
    (*LSB* 543:3–4)

And so, sing on, even now. Join the choir that hears His words for us and gives thanks for His endless forgiveness.

DISCUSSION QUESTIONS

1. When have you wanted to crank up the volume of your music and have needed bigger speakers?

2. This chapter talked about the voices that we so easily hear with their words of accusation from our past. Why do we listen so often to those distant voices that condemn us?

3. I described forgiveness as a powerful sound, a set of speakers for the whole campus or a band filling the whole gym with sound. When does forgiveness need to overwhelm the other sounds of your life?

4. From Romans 5:20–21, we noted that where sin increased, there grace increased all the more. How does God's grace more than match any increase in sin?

5. Romans 8:34 describes the intercession of the Son for our sake. What is reassuring about His ongoing words on our behalf?

6. The chapter described a concert where you are invited onto the stage to sing with the artist or band. With whom would you want to sing?

7. When God brings you into the song of forgiveness that He sings to the world, how is He using your voice to reach someone in particular?

One

You have to run to the grocery store for the chicken breasts, tomato sauce, and frozen corn you should have remembered when you were there yesterday. You park, run in, and are back out in ten minutes.

As you walk toward your car, you see a silver Lexus sedan back out of its spot, cross twenty feet of open space, and keep going straight back into your driver's side door. Your faithful Honda crumples like a soda can. When it can't go any farther back, the Lexus drives forward three feet and parks.

As you run to your car, a teenage boy gets out of the driver's side of the Lexus and his father gets out through the passenger door. They immediately go to the back of their car. Amazingly, the Lexus is perfect. The bumper isn't dented and there isn't even any blue paint from your Honda on it. The father looks at his car and says, "Whew, that was close. But it all looks okay." Then he turns to his son, who is looking confused as to how your Honda got in his way. The father asks him, "You feeling all right, Tony?" The boy says, "Yeah, sure, I'm okay."

The father then says, "Okay, well, good. Come on, let's go. We're already a little late."

They walk to the Lexus and are about to get in. They're going to drive away! Could this actually be?

You run in front of the Lexus and stand three feet in front of their bumper. They look at you, amazed. You're in their way. They can't understand it. So you explain.

"You're not going anywhere! I don't care if your car is fine. Look at my car! Look at what you did!"

The father says, "Well, you need to be more careful where you park. If you hadn't been parked there, none of this would have happened. It's just a good thing that Tony is okay."

You almost shout, "It's not my fault! It's yours! My car was parked in a parking space! You drove into me! My door's ruined! You're not getting away with this! Someone's got to pay!"

Have you felt this way? Your door was crumpled or your bumper dented and someone just drove away. There was no note left under your windshield wiper. Not even a "Sorry" written in the dust of your rear window. They just drove into you—and they knew they hit something—and they drove away. Someone's got to pay!

But it's more than a dented door. That door is a perfect example of sin as a trespass. The Lord's Prayer speaks of forgiving those who trespass against us, those who step into our space. The Lexus trespasses into your door, and you can see the bumper print that it left behind. The Lexus might drive away, but your door will never be the same.

Are there trespassing footprints left behind in your life? Does your front yard show the tracks of a frontal assault on your life? Those marks are set like footprints in concrete. Or is the trespassing trail hidden under the bushes? The bushes are doing their best to cover it all, but they can't completely hide the past. Even in the dark, you know exactly where the trespassing happened.

Those who left their footsteps behind have already gone away. You couldn't get in front of them as fast as you wanted. I wonder if they would have stopped anyway, or if they would have just flattened you if you had stayed there. Regardless, you're left with their footprints and the lasting memories of what was done to you.

All through this book, we've been talking about forgiveness, including forgiving those who have trespassed against us. But has that left you wondering about the question of this chapter: who's going to pay for this? Someone's got to pay, don't they? Or is forgiveness just a Lexus driving away from the accident? Is it just a father and son laughing about the dented doors behind them, asking each other, "Can you believe those people? They thought we should have to pay? What were they thinking? Don't they know who we are?"

Forgiveness might seem that way. It could be misunderstood as a painless drive from the scene of a crime. What if God simply watched the crumpled world from the comfort of an untouchable heaven? What if the most we could imagine was God seeing the damage in our world and saying a half-hearted "That's too bad. You're going to want to get that fixed, I suppose."

If all God cares about is the quiet of a perfect heaven, then maybe this world is not His problem. It's like your mother coming into the room just after your brother kicked you in the shin really hard. Now you're ready to give him back the same. But Mom says, "Don't you dare! Just let it go." But she's not the one hurting. You are! Of course, Mom's going to say, "Just walk away." Just walk away—that's easy when you're not the one who's limping.

Is that all God is saying when He commands, "If one has a complaint against another, [forgive] each other; as the Lord has forgiven you, so you also must forgive" (Colossians 3:13)? Is this an airy demand from God who says, "I've forgiven you and I'm fine with that. So, you should be too"? Is it only the words of a mother who was bothered by your shout when your brother kicked you? She has forgiven you for distracting her. Now you forgive your brother. Is that how forgiveness works? We've bothered God, but that's all right. He's decided to forgive and so He tells us to just let it go. Forgive.

But you're still hurting. Your shin really hurts. Your car door will never be the same. The bushes you planted won't cover up the trespasses from the past. You have to live with the pain, the dents, and the memories. Is forgiveness really this easy for others? Just an airy "That's all right. Fine. Drive off. I'm okay"?

GOOD NEWS: FORGIVENESS FOUND SOMEONE WHO'LL PAY

The good news of this chapter is that forgiveness is not an empty "Fine, just go. Don't worry about me." God knows our pain. Forgiveness isn't just a command from an untouched God, safe in heaven. Forgiveness comes from the One who knows pain and loss on a level we can't imagine. Someone has to pay, and someone already has.

SOMEONE HAS TO PAY, AND SOMEONE ALREADY HAS.

Remember the story of the father and son about to drive away? The father was concerned about his son above all. The image of a father protecting and valuing his son is the key. Of course, in the story, the father should also care about you and your car. But let's focus on God the Father and His Son and the value God puts on His only Son, Jesus. The power and possibility of forgiveness is found in this love. Jesus is the single, beloved Son, and so, through Him, God has taken on our sins, our pain, and the payment we needed. The value of that payment is found in the love of God for His only Son.

The payment for our sins comes with a balance of judgment and grace. In Romans 3, Paul explains that God can be both the loving parent and the righteous judge. He can both extract justice and give forgiveness:

> For all have sinned and fall short of the glory of God, and are justified by His grace as a gift, through the redemption that is in Christ Jesus, whom God put forward as a propitiation by His blood, to be received by faith. This was to show God's righteousness, because in His divine forbearance He had passed over former sins.

It was to show His righteousness at the present time, so
that He might be just and the justifier of the one who
has faith in Jesus. (Romans 3:23–26)

By this combination of judgment and grace, God hears our
pain with its cry for justice while also bringing us forward to forgiveness. He knows that someone has to pay, and that someone is
His innocent Son. The perfect Son will pay for
the collisions caused by all His wayward children. If someone injured by sin cries out, "Hey,
who's going to pay for this?" God can answer
that. He quietly says only this: "Pay? You need someone to pay?
I killed My Son for this. Is that payment enough for you?" Of
course, it is more than enough. What debt is not covered by that?

**IS THAT PAYMENT
ENOUGH FOR YOU?**

How do you hear God say those sentences? When God says,
"I killed My Son for this. Is that payment enough for you?" does
He shout with a deafening volume? I don't think so. I hear the
weary tone of a heartsore Father. This is the quiet of Good Friday's
darkness as the final hour draws near. The Father gives His Son
while we watch in awe. Our question of needing payment came
from our hurts and our losses. Our shin still hurts and our car door
is still dented. But those injuries don't seem nearly as important as
they once did. Can you seriously complain about how your shin
hurts while He hangs from the nails of the cross? Are you going
to go on about your dented door while you see a soldier plunge a
spear into His side? Then when the Father asks, "Is this enough
for you?" we instantly say, "Yes, yes, of course. I don't know what
I was thinking. This is more than enough."

This calm, brief word is perhaps surprising as our last side of
forgiveness. In the previous facet, we heard the many, many words
of Jesus as He interceded for us. We can imagine the words and
groanings too deep for words by the Spirit. Many are their words
and appeals for us. We pictured this as a crescendo of sound, so

powerful that we dared our enemies to match Him. God's words and sheer volume overwhelm those who accuse us. God answers those accusations with an avalanche of sound that surrounds us perfectly.

Shouldn't that eternal, almost deafening sound be the final image of forgiveness? It certainly could be, and we'll give a prominent place to this in our final chapter. But let's consider the power of a single, gentle word. It was the simple, quiet word of Nathan that completely undid David. After David's adultery and murder, Nathan told him the story of the rich man who killed the poor man's lamb. David raged against this cruelty, but Nathan brought him to his own sin with these few words: "You are the man." How do you overwhelm a murderous king? Tell him a simple story. Give him a mirror to see himself.

The power of the small word comes perhaps even more clearly with the experience of Elijah at the cave. The discouraged Elijah was promised that God would pass by him. But God was not in the mighty rushing wind, nor the earthquake, nor the fire. But then, "after the fire the sound of a low whisper. And when Elijah heard it, he wrapped his face in his cloak and went out and stood at the entrance of the cave" (1 Kings 19:12–13). God's small voice, so unexpected, so commanding, undid Elijah's defenses and disappointment. It drew him forward in awe. It is the small, quiet voice of God that calls us to walk with Him.

This small, quiet word fills the void as no explosion of sound could. There is a finality to the still voice that calms us and lets us know that He is God (Psalm 46:10). It is a bit like going to a Fourth of July fireworks show. The show has no set length and so you expect the show to last ten to fifteen minutes, at least here in our small towns. There's usually a crescendo of sound near the end as the explosions pile onto one another. The largest ones spread across the sky and then the little, intense ones come in rapid-fire succession. They build up until there's an intense thirty seconds of crashing colors. Then it's done. The smoke drifts away and we look at each other and say, "Is that it? Are they done?" It's not that we're complaining. We're just wondering if there's going to be any more because if not, we should start folding up the chairs and getting to the car.

Isn't that a strange ending to a wonderful show? Lights spread across the sky with ear-pulsing sound. Our senses have everything they could want. For a little town, this is very expensive. It's beautiful and it's only once a year. But as soon as it's over, we ask, "Is that it? Nothing more?"

Wouldn't it be easy for us to ask the same of God if we were to see the heavenly explosions and the demonstrations of His words for us? Because we read of it in Romans 8, we take by faith the promise that Jesus and the Spirit speak for us. What wonderful, endless words they speak for us all. But I fear that if we were to hear them, we might ask the same question: "Is that it? Is that all?" The problem of abundance is that it creates an endless hunger for more. More always demands more. Given paradise,

MORE ALWAYS DEMANDS MORE.

Adam and Eve still desired the one fruit they couldn't have. If we were to hear all that God says for us, we might somehow seek more.

More insists on finding more, but sometimes, a little is more than enough. So, the final word of God is the simple sentence of a man who spent Himself on the cross. It's the final word of a Father who gave up His Son. The last song He sings to us is not with the full choir and the orchestra at its greatest volume. No, His encore is something unexpected.

It's like going to a wonderful concert. The band has played for two hours, and the last song was wonderful. We clapped and cheered, hoping for an encore. Despite all we've heard, we want more. Now, let the singer come back onto the stage alone. The band is done, exhausted. The backup singers have not one note left in them. But the lead, the man we came to hear, he comes back onto the stage alone. He is so empty. He has no voice left and yet here he is. He sits on a stool, strums his guitar slow and sweet, and sings one final, simple song. His voice cracks. He whispers half of one verse and does the closing chorus only once while the crowd quietly helps him finish. When that chorus is done, he is done as well. He has nothing left. We won't ask for anything more. With that last, whispered song, he has given it all.

And so, God has one final song. When we ask for an encore at the concert of forgiveness, God the Father comes alone. Glorious angel choirs and uncounted armies of heavenly saints aren't needed. Let the Father take us back to that Good Friday afternoon and stand with us in the darkness. Let's stand quietly and watch as best we can when the world turns dark. Let's hear only Jesus' troubled breathing, and then let the Father say these words to us: "Did you ask for something more? Was there something else you needed to see? Look here. Listen. I gave My Son to die. And He did. So, let Me ask you, is that enough for you?" Yes, that is enough. That will always be enough.

RETRACE HIS STEPS

Hearing the Father ask that question gives us a new focus as we turn to forgive others as we've been forgiven. There are three steps to this forgiveness, a rather natural sequence. If we're actually going to forgive, we first need something new to fill our mind. We won't just forget what happened to us. Making our mind a vacuum will only invite the memories to refill the void. We can't change the past into nothing. It wasn't nothing. It was serious and it hurt. The only way we can forgive is when our mind is filled with another story besides our own. Only when we first remember can we hope to forget. We forget when we remember a story that's more memorable than our own.

ONLY WHEN WE FIRST REMEMBER CAN WE HOPE TO FORGET.

Remember the car accident in the parking lot? Let's join the story again where we left it. You're standing in front of the Lexus, asking, "Who's going to pay for this?" Holding the father and son in place, you call 911 and report the accident. For the sake of our story, the patrol car comes almost immediately and the officer asks what happened.

You're going to retrace all the steps. You walk the officer through each moment—coming out of the store, seeing the Lexus back out, watching it crunch in your door then pull ahead, the two of them getting out, looking at the bumper, getting back in their car, and trying to leave. You'll act out every step, ending up with you once again standing in front of the Lexus, holding it in place. You'll end the story by saying, "There, that's what happened. I dare you to say it didn't."

We want to trace the steps of those who trespass against us. No matter how long ago it was, we can follow that ancient trail. Those footprints might be too old for anyone else to see them, but we can see those prints perfectly. Not only can we see the trespasses—we can tell their story. Every time we recount what happened, we draw the outline of each step a bit deeper. We retrace each trespass and say, "There, that's what happened. I dare you to say it didn't."

> "THERE, THAT'S WHAT HAPPENED. I DARE YOU TO SAY IT DIDN'T."

There's only one way to forgive those steps. Retrace His steps instead. Tell His story once again to yourself. When you begin to retrace those same old trespassing steps, remind yourself of the steps He took and the trespasses that were pressed on Him. Paul captures this with his advice on how we can possibly live humbly with one another:

> Do nothing from rivalry or conceit, but in humility count others more significant than yourself. . . . Have this mind among yourselves, which is yours in Christ

> Jesus, who, though He was in the form of God, did
> not count equality with God a thing to be grasped, but
> made Himself nothing, taking the form of a servant,
> being born in the likeness of men. And being found
> in human form, He humbled Himself by becoming
> obedient to the point of death, even death on a cross.
> (Philippians 2:3, 5–8)

How does your story compare to His? How do your scars look compared to His? How many angry voices calling for your crucifixion are in your story? When we start to tell His story, ours begins to shrink. Ours is true, but it's so small compared to His. Trace His story with the same passion and detail that you would use to tell your sharpest trespass story. Tell His story and then ask yourself, "Now what was I saying about what happened to me?" It's a small turn on the words of Paul, "For I consider that the sufferings of this present time are not worth comparing with the glory that is to be revealed to us" (Romans 8:18). Perhaps we might also say that the sufferings of our past and present time are also not worth comparing to the suffering of Christ for our sake and the glory that He will share with us. Trace His steps and tell His story. You'll be surprised what happens to your story when you do.

COUNT HIS COST

After you get done telling the story to the patrolman, walking out the exact steps that the Lexus took, next you'll start to count the cost. You'll say to the patrolman, "Look at this door! Do you know how much this is going to cost? These people"—pointing to the father and son—"don't seem to care. And you know, that door will never be the same again. They never get it back to new."

Counting the cost is the natural second step after telling the story. In fact, counting the cost takes more time. You have to figure the money for the deductible, the lost time and wages for

ONE

you to bring the car in for the estimates, and then the days you'll be without your car. How much will it cost to Uber to work all those days? And you just know that you'll remember this every time you open that driver's door. The paint won't be quite the same. The door handle won't open and close quite as well. There's going to be a strange sound whistling from around the window. The cost? It's more than a few hundred for the deductible. You'll be counting that cost for a long time.

That's another question we have about forgiveness. Has God counted the cost? If we forgive someone, who's going to pay? And don't forget, that cost keeps on and on. Some of the trespasses we're forgiving started small, but their cost is still going on today. It's the relationship that has never been the same. It's the job that you could have had but now never will. It's the health you might have enjoyed, but now it's gone. What's the cost of all that? And who's going to pay?

Count His cost. Just as tracing His steps gives you an alternative story to the trespasses against you, so counting His cost gives you a new ledger to focus on compared to the column of debts owed to you. Consider His journey and the cost that it brought Him. The writer to the Hebrews captured this idea in describing our race, following Jesus as the one who ran before us: "Let us run with endurance the race that is set before us, looking to Jesus, the founder and perfecter of our faith, who for the joy that was set before Him endured the cross, despising the shame, and is seated at the right hand of the throne of God. Consider Him who endured from sinners such hostility against Himself, so that you may not grow weary or fainthearted" (12:1–3).

Consider His cost. It's like being stuck on the highway but then thinking of someone else. Holly and I visited our daughter Christy at her home in Alexandria, Virginia. It's a one-day, 850-mile drive back to Wisconsin, so we left at 5:00 a.m. By 5:05, we were on the 495 Beltway, heading north. In a minute, traffic came to a halt.

125

All three lanes were full and stopped. We never moved an inch for the next three hours and forty minutes. A woman had been killed in an accident just ahead of us. So, we all just waited. We got out of our cars. The boys ahead of us played football, and we met a very interesting woman who operated a construction crane. No one complained. Oh, we all had places to go. Appointments were missed and jobs were undone. But remember the woman who died. What was our problem compared to her family's that day? We still made it home to Wisconsin that evening. Count her cost, and our delay was nothing.

Count His cost. No question about it, you have lost a great deal through the trespasses of others. The compounded interest of those sins has grown every day. But adding it all up won't erase that ledger of debt. However, there is something you can do. Lay someone else's account on top of yours. Count His costs. Imagine the insults, the attacks on His words, and the outright lies He faced. List, if you can, the temptations He endured. Imagine all the times when He could have crushed His enemies but instead let them live, only to have them plot against Him. Listen with Him to the whispered plans to kill Him, and hear the jingle of the thirty pieces of silver handed to Judas. List it all if you can. Count His cost.

What a price He paid! While we can only barely imagine the whole cost that He bore, it comes down to that one sentence. Take the record of all He paid and put it next to that list of wrongs done to us. How do the two compare? As you look at those lists, hear His Father say, "I saw My Son suffer. I watched Him die. I did nothing to stop it. It was all for you. Is that enough?" Count the cost paid by the Son.

YOUR LEDGER OF DEBT WILL BE LOST WHEN HIS LIES ON TOP.

Count the cost of a heartbroken Father. Your ledger of debt will be lost when His lies on top.

Remember. He Forgets.

When you trace His steps and count His cost, something begins to happen to your own story. All that happened to you is still there. But something else becomes more important. His story takes over. His death and His resurrection become the story on which we focus. When that happens, we remember Him and begin to forget the trespasses against us.

It's like the time I was driving my Model A Ford one November evening. My father and I restored a 1930 Model A Ford car over the course of four years. We'd already restored a 1917 Model T Ford car, and the Model A was a way to continue our partnership. When it was done, I drove the Model A eleven thousand miles in three years around our small town of Butternut, Wisconsin. One late November afternoon, as the sun was setting, I was coming home. Suddenly, the engine stopped running and I coasted to a stop on the side of a county road, five miles from home. My dark blue Model A didn't have turn signals or warning lights, and I was stuck there, cold, dark, and a little lonely.

I knew what was likely the problem. The gas tank was rusty, and though I had tried cleaning it many times, it continued to send rust and grit down the gas line to the carburetor. The two standard Ford gas filters didn't stop the grit, which, like tiny stones, clogged the main jet in the carb. Once the jet was blocked, the engine stopped.

Two thousand pounds of car, carefully restored, could be stopped by a tiny piece of rust. All my plans and schedule were at the mercy of this tiny stone. I needed to open the carburetor and clean it out, but I also needed light. Tools I had, but foolishly, I didn't have a flashlight.

Then came a really big flashlight. A logging truck came down the road and, fortunately, saw me in time to pull up behind me. I went to the cab and explained the problem. The driver kindly volunteered to stay and shine his lights toward the Model A. So, I got out a wrench and removed the one bolt that held the carburetor together so I could get to the main and pilot jets. Ideally, in the shop, I would have used the air compressor to blow out the jets, but that night I could only puff at them myself. After a few puffs, I would have liked to see if they were clear, but it was much too dark. All I could do was trust that the stone had been removed. I bolted the carb together, turned the gas on, and tried the starter. It started right up. The stone was gone.

I went back to the trucker, thanked him, and watched him drive off. I got back in the Model A and drove home. That was one of the best drives I ever had with that Model A. I loved listening to that patient old Ford engine puttering along. Now, it wasn't a perfect car. My dad and I weren't professional body men, and so there were a few dents not completely worked out. I painted the car in our garage and it was good, but not perfect. I drove it a lot and it had a scratch or two on it. And the gas tank still had rust. But did I worry about any of that on the ride home? Absolutely not! That car had died and it was alive again. I had been stuck on the side of the road, completely vulnerable to every unseeing driver who might come along. But now I was rolling again, lights shining, heading home. What was a dent, a scratch, a little rust? Nothing. All those things, every scratch and dent, could be added up, and yet their sum was nothing compared to one simple truth: the car was dead but now it was running. That engine running was worth far more than everything else. It was all because the stone had moved.

IT WAS ALL BECAUSE THE STONE HAD MOVED.

The stone has moved for us all. The stone in the carburetor was tiny, but it stopped everything. It's that way with another stone, the one that affects us all. The stone that was in front of Jesus' tomb was no mountain, but it could've stopped the world. Compared to the enormity of the Rocky Mountains, the stone in front of Jesus' tomb was a pebble. But look what it stopped. If that stone were to stay in place and Jesus were to remain dead behind that stone, then the world would have been doomed. Paul said it well: "If Christ has not been raised, your faith is futile and you are still in your sins. Then those also who have fallen asleep in Christ have perished. If in Christ we have hope in this life only, we are of all people most to be pitied" (1 Corinthians 15:17–19).

But the stone has moved. Easter's joy is the absence of the stone and the emptiness of the tomb. All this takes faith. On the side of the road in the dark, I would never see the stone leave the carburetor jet. I could only trust, bolt the carb together, and try to start the engine. Faith alone trusts that in the predawn darkness, Christ rose, and the stone, when moved, showed there was nothing behind it. We can't see the resurrection moment of Jesus leaving the tomb. But we who once were dead are alive. Joined as we are to Christ through Baptism, we're on the Easter side of the stone. "We were buried therefore with Him by baptism into death, in order that, just as Christ was raised from the dead by the glory of the Father, we too might walk in newness of life" (Romans 6:4).

This changes our daily drive. I expect that we've all accumulated more than one scratch, tear, and dent. We're behind schedule and we'll never catch up. The list of wrongs done against us are a whole set of dents done by those who want to drive away. But what does it matter? We were dead but now we're alive. "God, being rich in mercy, because of the great love with which He loved us, even when we were dead in our trespasses, made us alive together with Christ" (Ephesians 2:4–5). That one truth more than balances out every perfection that's ruined and every problem we haven't fixed. Now we're alive through a restart that won't be stopped. My gas tank was always a bit rusty, but a third gas filter finally stopped those little pieces from getting to the carb. I was never stranded on the road again. But our life is even more secure. God who has raised us from the dead has already placed us with Himself in heaven. "[God] raised us up with Him and seated us with Him in the heavenly places in Christ Jesus, so that in the coming ages

He might show the immeasurable riches of His grace in kindness toward us in Christ Jesus" (Ephesians 2:6–7).

The stone has moved. Once dead but now alive, we will never die again. Jesus says it with reassuring directness: "Truly, truly, I say to you, whoever hears My word and believes Him who sent Me has eternal life. He does not come into judgment, but has passed from death to life" (John 5:24). Our eternity has begun even while we wait for more. I drove home that night knowing that I would have to do something about that gas tank so I wouldn't be stopped again. That third filter would come later in the garage. But for those five miles that evening, it was more than enough just to be running again. What I had to do someday didn't take away the joy of what I got to do that night. I simply drove my old friend, the Model A, home.

Aren't we the same right now? Are there things that need a lasting fix about you and your life? Absolutely, and they're more significant than a rusty gas tank. We have real problems that need a final fix. When we're made new in the resurrection, those problems will finally be fixed. We'll leave to Him the time and the manner of that resurrection and all it'll bring. For now, we have this one truth, a single sentence, which is more than enough. He is alive and so are we in a living faith. Despite our frailties, we who were dead are alive. No one will take us out of His hand and nothing will separate us from His love. That connection by His power is our life. Since it depends on Him, it won't stop or fail. Let all the failures of life, all the scratches, dents, and delays, be added up. They will never be as important as this one word: alive.

THEY WILL NEVER BE AS IMPORTANT AS THIS ONE WORD: ALIVE.

When we remember that we're alive, we can forget. When we remember that He forgets our sins, we begin to forgive and forget. In the concordance section of *The Lutheran Study Bible*, you'll find a wonderful collection of words, appearing in this order, with no other words intruding: *forgave, forget, forgets, forgetting, forgive, forgiven, forgiveness, forgives, forgiving, forgot, forgotten.* Perhaps there's a connection between forgiving and forgetting. Of course, the Hebrew and Greek words underlining the ideas of forgiveness and forgetting don't appear alphabetically side by side. But in English, it's a wonderful sequence as we weave back and forth between the two ideas. God forgives and He also forgets. Remember the powerful images of His removing sins from us. "He will again have compassion on us; He will tread our iniquities underfoot. You will cast all our sins into the depths of the sea" (Micah 7:19). Here's another image of God's forgetting: "In love You have delivered my life from the pit of destruction, for You have cast all my sins behind Your back" (Isaiah 38:17). God forgives all our debt as did the king in the parable of the debtor who owed ten thousand talents. The king forgave the debt because the man desperately asked for mercy. However, when the servant did not forgive the much, much smaller debt owed to him by another man, the king said, "You wicked servant! I forgave you all that debt because you pleaded with me. And should not you have had mercy on your fellow servant, as I had mercy on you?" (Matthew 18:32–33). The message is clear: Remember. He forgets.

Surprising How It Turned Out

Let's go back to the story of the accident with the Lexus. I don't have much hope for that father and son. They seem a bit too self-absorbed to make a happy ending for you. I do have hope for the patrolman though. He agrees with you completely. He writes up the son for the accident and gathers the father's insurance information for you. The father's insurance is going to pay for the damages, and the patrolman tells you that if there is any problem with this, you're to give him a call. He leaves you his card with all his contact information. He was wonderful, and you end up remembering him more than anything else from that day.

How does the message of forgiveness leave us? It depends on our focus. If we only trace the trespasses done against us, we'll never get over the costs that keep building. Forgiveness? If we hear that word, we've got one hard question: "See all this. Who's going to pay?"

But against that growing ledger of debt, God has His own story to tell and His own steps to trace. Against the crescendo of complaints we have against the world, He has a few quiet words. His story is enough and His costs are staggering when we see them. When we tell His story instead of ours and count His costs instead of ours, forgiveness becomes the final song we can't forget. Then we come with the hope that He has forgotten our sins as well as those who trespass against us. In the end, dare to ask the heavenly Father, "Who's going to pay?" Then listen as He quietly says, "I gave up My Son. I watched Him die and did nothing to stop it. I gave you My Son. Is that enough for you?" Yes, that was enough, more than enough, for all of us.

NORTHERN RED OAK—ONE TREE WILL DO

As I described it in chapter 6, red oak is the king of the cabinet and furniture woods. It is beautiful, strong, and versatile. It's the door you open, the floor you walk on, and the furniture you rest on. As I mentioned, it's the floor of our enormous chapel. There are some 327,375 pieces to our parquet floor, beautifully holding us all up for almost sixty years now with no end in sight.

But all those pieces, too many to count, can also be reduced to one. For this panel on the cube, we have again red oak, but only one piece instead of the many parquet pieces from the previous chapter. The largest red oak tree in Wisconsin stands 85 feet tall with a circumference of 226 inches. Online sources give different formulas to determine the yield of a tree, though a tree of this size is often off the charts. If this giant were ever milled for lumber, it's safe to say it would yield thousands of square feet of lumber. Our chapel floor is plywood with a veneer of red oak. The surface that we see and walk on is only an eighth of an inch thick. So, take that one oak tree, slice it thin at the veneer mill, and you would have all the red oak needed to cover our chapel floor. One tree could do it all.

What was countless can be reduced to one. As we noted in chapter 6, the almost countless pieces of flooring could be missed. But you would never miss one towering tree. The words of Jesus for us are so many, we can't count them. But all those words speak of only one tree. The cross is the tree that yields all that we stand on. The cross is the unmistakable tree. The cross is the tree that towers over the world and cannot be missed or forgotten. The cross is the one tree that will be more than enough for all.

RED—THE COLOR WE SEE BUT ONCE

We can wear out the green paraments and stoles. After all, they're used for about half the year, so they're the first to become frayed. Opposite the green is red. Red is the color for Pentecost, the day when we remember the tongues of fire above the disciples' heads. Red is the color we won't wear out. Put it on the altar, and we'll all notice that something rare and special is happening.

Certainly, red is the right color for our final theme. One single act saves us all. The blood of Jesus cleanses us and gives us God's peace. Red is the color of His Father's gift to the world. When the Father gives us His quiet, simple words, let them be written in red. Let His words echo in our minds: "I gave you My Son. I gave Him to die. Is that enough for you?"

HYMNS OF FORGIVENESS

This chapter has heard God's all-sufficient Word, said with quiet power. A perfect hymn for this is "A Mighty Fortress Is Our God." Let all the devil's words and power come against us. God's single word is more than enough:

> Though devils all the world should fill,
>   All eager to devour us,
>
> We tremble not, we fear no ill;
>   They shall not overpow'r us.
>
> This world's prince may still
>   Scowl fierce as he will,
>
> He can harm us none.
>   He's judged; the deed is done;
>
> One little word can fell him. (*LSB* 656:3)

Another hymn by Martin Luther also stresses the all-sufficient gift of Jesus and the price of this gift. "Dear Christians, One and All, Rejoice" describes the love of the Father who forgave us by the costliest gift:

> But God had seen my wretched state
>   Before the world's foundation,
>
> And mindful of His mercies great,
>   He planned for my salvation.
>
> He turned to me a father's heart;
>   He did not choose the easy part
>
> But gave His dearest treasure. (*LSB* 556:4)

One word, one gift. When it is the Word who is the Father's only Son, then that One is all we need. Our forgiveness rests safely on that One alone.

DISCUSSION QUESTIONS

1. The chapter begins with the story of an accident. How would you react if you watched your car get hit and the other driver seemed ready to just drive away?

2. The chapter described the enormous sound of the concert and the fireworks. As wonderful as the final song was, and as stunning as the final barrage of fireworks might be, how are we sometimes left asking for more?

3. When God tells us to forgive, why might we first want to retell the story of the trespasses that were made against us?

4. Besides retelling the story of what was done wrong to us, how do we also try to calculate the cost of those trespasses?

5. But to that story and cost, the chapter says, "Trace His steps and count His cost." What steps of Jesus most often come to your mind? What were some of the costs that He took on?

6. The chapter pictured the Father quietly saying, "I gave you My Son. Is that enough for you?" How are that simple gift and single question enough for us?

7. The last two chapters used red oak twice, once for the floor of our chapel and once for the single tree that would yield all those pieces. Which image of the work of God comes to mind for you most often: the countless individual gifts of God's grace or the single tree of the cross?

There's More to Forgiveness than the Cube: Did You See It Coming?

olly and I enjoy watching mysteries on TV in the evening. Throughout the show, we're wondering who the murderer is. The angry former employee or the ex-husband is always a good bet. But it should be more than a blind guess or a simple "I don't like him." Usually, there's some clue that we're supposed to have noticed and, if we do, then we can be as certain as Jethro Gibbs or Jessica Fletcher. Of course, all this requires that we stay awake while we're watching. Unfortunately, we don't always make it through the show. Then we're back to guessing whether it was the ex-wife or the shifty-looking neighbor.

You're probably better at this than we are. You stay awake through the whole show and have it figured out after twenty minutes. But even if we take a quick nap halfway through, the show will tell us the answer in the end. It's much the same here with chapter 8. You maybe saw this chapter coming when we first starting making our cube of forgiveness with its three pairs. A cube is certainly a handy way to display three pairs of opposing ideas. I'm not sure there's any other shape that would do it. But maybe you thought that there could be more to the cube than just three sets of pairs.

One factor in this is how you make your cube. I see two different methods. One is the wooden cube I've been describing. The six different wood panels are glued to an underlying solid wooden cube. It's sanded smooth and shines with a tung oil finish. The cube is as sturdy and unchanging as forgiveness itself.

But the cube showing the six colors could be made out of paper. When presenting the ideas of this book to classes, I make these cubes out of thick poster board with crumbled paper stuffed in the center, just to give it some body. Then I give each small group the paper cube and markers in the six colors of our study. As we go through each facet, I have each group color that facet. This will be one of our discussion questions in this unit, but you can start to think about it now. Besides the colors of white, black, purple, blue, green, and red, what small symbols tell the story of each facet of forgiveness? I suggest a nail for the Fixed panel and perhaps a bowl of water for Clean. But don't let me curb your creativity.

Once you have that paper cube decorated and colored, it's time for the final step. Do with the paper cube what you can't with the wooden one. Take it apart. If you've made the cube out of one piece of paper, you have only one shape: the cross! You'll have a cross made of four vertical panels and two horizontal panels attached to the second vertical panel from the top. (I wish I could say that I saw the cube/cross combination from the start, but I must have been sleeping through the whole process. I wrote up the six facets of forgiveness and then thought of putting together cubes for class. Only when I was cutting out the cubes from poster board did it hit me. It's a cross! You saw this much sooner, I'm sure.)

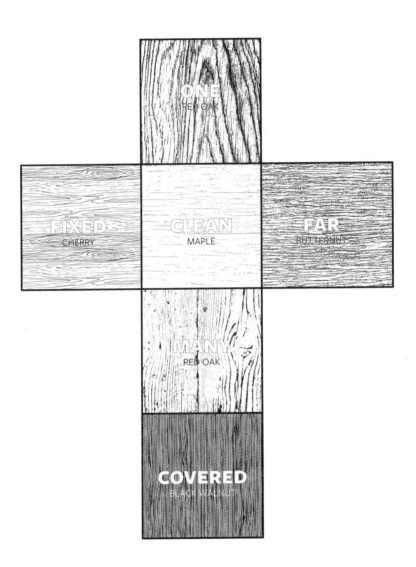

LET'S ARRANGE THE PANELS

Here is where I wish we could be together and unfold the cube as a group project. When I do this with a Bible class, I number the panels on the cube and then direct the class to fill in the panels in the order I've numbered them. That way, everyone's cross turns out the same. However, if I let you do it in any set of opposing pairs, then your pattern will be different. For the body of this chapter, we'll go with my suggested design, but yours might well be better.

Let's start in the middle of the cross with the panel that is the junction between the vertical and the horizontal. I put Clean there as the most central image of forgiveness. As we noted in chapter 2, the cleansing of sin expresses our desire to start over again as new people. God's cleansing shows His creative power and also His enduring choice to see us always as His perfect Bride. I like the central position to be Clean since it is the meeting place of the vertical and horizontal. Here, the almost-white of the maple wood wards off any stain. This panel is the place of resolution between opposites so that when the stain and the cleansers meet, the whiteness of the Clean panel results.

It's a bit like the result of the cross as seen between Pilate and Herod. Pilate heard that Jesus was from Galilee, and so he sent Jesus to be examined by Herod. Herod had been seeking to examine Jesus, and so Herod questioned Jesus, though Jesus said nothing. Despite this, it changed the relationship between Herod and Pilate. "Herod and Pilate became friends with each other that very day, for before this they had been at enmity with each other" (Luke 23:12).

This is what the cross does. The cross is the greatest intersection the world has ever known. On the cross, the One who is both God and man dies. He bridges heaven and earth so that they meet on the vertical plane of the cross. But when Christ is upon the cross, He also joins the most dissimilar people on earth, since He came for all people. Imagine two people who are complete opposites, and yet even their sins are cleansed equally on the cross. Let the two distant horizontal arms of the cross remind us that the sins of all are brought together and cleansed on the cross.

What a radiant center the cross is. The cleansing of forgiveness brings the greatest breadth of people together. Perhaps we can glimpse this in Revelation with the gathering of heaven:

> After this I looked, and behold, a great multitude that no one could number, from every nation, from all tribes and peoples and languages, standing before the throne and before the Lamb, clothed in white robes. . . . Then one of the elders addressed me, saying, "Who are these, clothed in white robes, and from where have they come?" I said to him, "Sir, you know." And he said to me, "These are the ones coming out of the great tribulation. They have washed their robes and made them white in the blood of the Lamb." (7:9, 13–14)

Let this white center of our cross be the gathering of the most diverse people. They have lost their hostile distance and any competitive appearance. So, the gathering of every nation and tribe, with all their separate colors, come together clothed alike in the robes washed in the blood of the Lamb. They are united through the work of the cross. The cleansing of forgiveness brings them to the center of our salvation, the cross.

THE PANEL WE NEVER SEE

If we label the central panel as Clean, then the bottom panel will be Covered. This works very well if we assume this is the part of the cross that is driven into the ground. This is the forgotten part of the cross, and forgetting is a key part of God's covering. This panel is colored black in our structure and made of black walnut. Both of these choices fit the role of the covering of sins.

Black walnut costs the most of all the woods that I've described. I rarely use it for any large project since it is so expensive. Award plaques are often made of black walnut since it's beautiful and should be displayed. On the other hand, would you build a dresser out of pine but make the hidden sections out of black walnut? Try explaining this plan to the lumberyard manager when you buy the walnut. Tell him your idea. "I'm only going to use the walnut for the runners underneath the drawer. No one will ever see it. So, can I get a discount?" The lumberman will seriously wonder about you and, no, there's no discount. Beautiful, expensive walnut should not be hidden.

Where would you put the wondrous Son of God? When He shines like the sun in His moments of transfiguration, He's on a mountain, but He's seen by only three men. But when He is on the cross, we see Him through every cross ever made. But yet, that day was shrouded in black for the last three hours. When He gives His life, the world is in darkness. His gift is given in the dark to a world that largely refused to recognize Him even in the light.

But in that darkness, He buries our sins. As amazing as the gift of the precious Son is, it is equally fitting that some part of the cross be completely buried beneath the surface. Let the cross be partially hidden as a reminder that He has likewise covered our sins. They are buried in the depth of the cross and in the darkness of the tomb. Our sins, once buried, will never break out as the thorns and thistles, witnessing against us. The cross has buried them and still bears down on them with all its weight.

IT IS A BEAUTY LEFT IN THE DARK, A MYSTERY TOO MARVELOUS TO UNCOVER.

So, bury that black walnut beneath the soil. Let the most expensive and beautiful part of the cross be largely hidden. The sacrifice of Jesus must largely remain a wonder and a mystery to us. We can't imagine all that He endured for us. It is a beauty left in the dark, a mystery too marvelous to uncover.

The Answer We Seek

Now that we have two panels on the vertical portion of the cross, let's turn to the horizontal arms of the cross. These become the pair of Fixed and Far. The horizontal bar of the cross with the outstretched arms of Jesus nailed there works very well for both of these ideas. The nails on the bar certainly speak of Fixed, while the breadth of the bar hints at the Far distance to which He has sent our sins. But there's a bit more to this horizontal bar when we consider the colors and wood.

When we ask God for forgiveness, we remember both the hurts that we've caused and those put onto us. We both regret and question the past. Wouldn't it have been better if some of those moments never happened? We would like to ask God, "Where were You? What were You doing when all this was going on? Why didn't You do something?"

Those are all good questions. Go ahead and ask them, especially when you see Jesus coming near to you as you sit crumpled on the floor. He stretches out His hand to hold yours, touches your most aching spot, and begins to lift you up. Go ahead. Ask Him, "Where were You? Why didn't You do something?"

Let the nail marks in His hand give the answer. The answer, at least as much as we might have in this world, is fixed by the nails. Let His wounds say, "I did do this much. When you're wondering where I was, I was here, fixed on the cross." He doesn't need to answer our questions, and likely we wouldn't be able to take the full answer if He gave it. Besides, why should the King answer every complaining question from His people? We made this panel purple, the royal color, and built it of cherry, that beautiful wood that turns to the richest red color. Now mark that beautiful wood with the deep piercing of a nail and let it turn even more

> **WHEN YOU'RE WONDERING WHERE I WAS, I WAS HERE, FIXED ON THE CROSS.**

red in that spot where you've opened the grain. Let that open nail hole remind us of His wounds. Let those wounds be His answer when we ask what God has done for us.

MAKE THIS ONE A BIT LONGER

The cross should be symmetrical, and when it's a cube unfolded, each panel has to be identical in size. But if I were to build a cross to show these six panels of forgiveness and didn't fold it into a cube, I would make this panel just a bit longer. Not twice the length, but just long enough that someone might possibly notice. Let them ask, "Ah, say, isn't that one side a little longer than the other? Not that it looks bad, but I was just wondering."

Yes, that's exactly the point. That's because the horizontal arm opposite Fixed is Far, and Far should be just a bit longer than its horizontal partner. The Fixed side isn't moving, but the idea of Far stretches itself out a bit. After all, where do we want our sins to be? This is opposite of the question we asked of the Fixed side. The Fixed side asked of God, "Where were You?" We don't want a distant God but one who is here, fixed in a place where we can reach. But now the question is the opposite: "Where are our sins, near or far?"

We want them to be far away, of course. Let our sins be on the most outstretched arm of the cross. Let it be out of proportion if it must be, but let that extended arm remind us that God has taken our sins far, far away. Remember that this panel is made of butternut, that beautiful wood that was the reason for our town's name. It was the place farthest north on the rail line where the butternut tree could be found. So, let this horizontal stretch of the cross remind you that God has done a beautiful work, but the effect of that work has taken our sins far out of reach.

That's why we used the color blue for this arm. Blue is the color of the outstretched heavens. Blue invites us to lift up our eyes to be reminded that our help is in Him who fills the heavens.

This wonderful panel of Far reminds us that while our sins are taken far out of our sight, the heavens are our home. The marks we've inflicted on others have been taken away by the harsher carving done by the cross's nails. But those nail marks are far from accusing us. He has put His wrath away and makes peace by His cross. Let the cross reassure you that sin's guilt has been put far, far away.

Springing out Ever Green

It's been a remarkable fall this year. As I write this, it's October 25 and we haven't had a frost yet. For Cedar Grove, Wisconsin, that's amazingly late. The lovely maple tree in our front yard has turned color and is dropping its leaves, but the grass around it is the deepest summer green you can imagine. Throw in the red and yellow mums Holly has in the window box and it's an explosion of color.

It's the maple tree growing out of that deep green that I want you to see. That green is the color for our tree, the cross, as the cross emerges from the ground. The black walnut of the very bottom panel is hidden in the darkness. But spreading upward is the green of the next panel. There's life where we would expect death. There's green grass still growing and needing to be mowed when we should have frost. There is life in this panel when the innocent Son comes back from the dead to speak on our behalf.

The joy of this panel is it never stops. Our lawn won't stop growing this week and our geraniums continue to bloom like it's July. What should be dead is alive. Isn't that the wonderful image of the cross where we hear the endless words of the resurrected Son speaking on our behalf? His words are countless in number and endless in time. Like a living tree, let this part of the cross be sturdy and even growing. The red oak we used here is perfect, since oak grows so readily and is found in so many places, and the parquet-floor arrangement further demonstrates the Many facet.

> **HIS WORDS ARE COUNTLESS IN NUMBER AND ENDLESS IN TIME.**

Let that sturdy oak be the assurance that the cross on which we depend will always stand.

It's How You Cut It

In the Northwoods, the sawyer is an important man. The sawyer runs the sawmill and directs how each log is cut. This is an art carefully learned through every log that he saws. A good sawyer has to see the beauty of the wood that is hidden under the bark. He has to guide the log through the saw in such a way as to get the most beautiful cuts while also using the greatest amount of the log. How he turns the log and the sequence of cuts he takes are going to decide the value of the boards.

Woodworkers will argue all day as to the best way to saw a log, but I especially like plain sawing, which results in cathedral grain. The grain of a plainsawn oak board often looks like an arch in a large building like a cathedral. It looks like two hands brought together with the tips of the fingers just touching. Picture your hands praying with the fingers pointing upward, fingertips just touching but not intertwined. You likely have a piece of oak or other wood that has this pattern. This final panel is focused on One—one gift, one sacrifice, and the one color red that commands our attention. The oak here is one piece, not the many pieces of the parquet arrangement in the Many panel. Let the image of hands reaching upward be the final image of our prayer and praise.

WHEN OUR FISTS ARE CLENCHED AND OUR WOUNDED HANDS ARE EMPTY, POINT THEM TO THE TOP OF THE CROSS.

Forgiveness has come with its many colors and shapes. It gives an answer to our demand that something has to be done about the injuries we've sustained. When our fists are clenched and our wounded hands are empty, point them to the top of the cross. See that cathedral grain stretching upward. When you're aching and empty, point upward to Him, the one who has given His Son on the cross. Find in the cross of Christ the final piece that is enough of an answer for our questions. Point upward to His heaven, marveling that He came from there to fill the cross, and by that, we have forgiveness in all its facets.

REMEMBER KELSEY'S RING?

We started the book with the story of Kelsey and Henry and their engagement ring. Kelsey is still happily wearing the ring and the wedding plans are going forward. I predict a wonderful marriage for them. Kelsey's going to cherish that ring for decades. It looks perfect today and will be just as bright on their fiftieth anniversary. I'm not sure they'll still be watching the same movie for their anniversary—how will we even watch movies fifty years from now?—but the ring will be just as beautiful.

That's the cube of forgiveness. It's the engagement of God with all His people. It's the priceless gem that endures. It has facets that are distinct, and yet each facet needs the others in order to be complete. Time cannot diminish the beauty of the forgiveness cube. In fact, the endurance of each facet makes it more beautiful. Each sin is cleaned and covered, fixed in place and moved out of sight, spoken over in the loudest tone and answered with one simple word. The sins of a lifetime cannot dull the facets of forgiveness. Sin can't hope to be harder than the diamond strength of God's work. Sin can't pry this diamond from us, since we're in His hands. Forgiveness is the hold He has on us.

Sin can't find a dimension that isn't answered in the variety of God's forgiveness. If we happen to stumble onto a new sin, we won't find one that can't be matched by God's forgiveness. Even if a new sin intrudes into our lives and our relationships, the facets of forgiveness have known it and answered it. The cube of forgiveness says, in an adaptation of Ecclesiastes, "Is there a thing of which it is said, 'See, this is new'? It has been already in the ages before us" (1:10). Forgiveness cleanses all sins, no matter the stain. Forgiveness can cover any sin with the life of Christ and the darkness of His death. Forgiveness is our reassurance, fixed as deeply as the nails driven into the cross. Forgiveness picks up the heaviest and most stubborn sin and hurls it beyond our sight and life. Forgiveness multiplies faster than even the worst sin as the endless words of Christ for us grow in volume. But in the end, forgiveness is the answer of the Father who can meet any challenge by the simple sentences "I gave you My Son. Is that enough for you?"

It is enough. Kelsey is thrilled to have the single diamond Henry picked out. She won't be asking for another. We have more than enough in the diamond of forgiveness. Blessings to you as you hold this cube and turn each facet to the light. Let each day's different light bring out a new color from each face. This is God's lasting engagement with us.

THE CUBE WE CAN'T SEE

We've made cubes from wood and paper, concentrating on the color and feel of each side. Now let's make one more cube, but this one is transparent. It's not the sides of the cube that will matter but what's inside the cube. My friend Dr. Nicole Muth, a math professor at Concordia University Wisconsin, does this demonstration with her students. Take a cube made of plastic straws with only the outer edges defined and the sides otherwise open. Immerse the cube in a solution of water and detergent. Lift the straw framework out of the solution and you'll have a transparent cube, shimmering sides with an empty middle. Now, take a straw dipped into the bubble solution, insert it through the cube wall, and blow a bubble inside the cube. Amazingly, the cube sides won't collapse, and the cube won't explode with the added air blown in. Instead, the air bubble is trapped inside the cube. Take out the straw and the bubble remains.

(By the way, Dr. Muth assures me that the internet has many examples of this demonstration.)

The cube of forgiveness is this shimmering cube. We might approach God tentatively with our confession, afraid that our entry into forgiveness will shatter God's perfect cube. Instead, God brings us to Himself so we can exhale our confession of sin. This long breath, this bubble of confession, is trapped within the cube of forgiveness. Our confession, however large, is held within the forgiveness of God. In the math experiment, you can look through the cube to see the bubble inside. The wonderful difference with God is that He alone knows our confession and He alone sees our sin. We can step from that exhale of confession with relief, leaving behind our confessed sins. The cube of God's forgiveness is not fragile or temporary but as sturdy as the nails and the cross. Come to His forgiveness, breathe out your confession, and know that He holds it forever, trapped within His forgiveness.

THE CROSS SOLVES THE PUZZLE

My friend Dr. Scott Van Ornum teaches chemistry at Concordia University Wisconsin. Scott has many interests including solving Rubik's Cube. When Scott learned of my cube theme for this book, he showed me how to solve Rubik's Cube using the cross. Now, I have never solved Rubik's Cube, not even close. But Scott can do it in just a few seconds—I've seen him! His method starts by making a cross on one face using the white panels. I'll leave to you math and science geniuses how to do this, but Scott can take the cube in any state and, with several quick twists, produce a cross, three pieces horizontal, three pieces vertical, meeting in the middle. Once he has the cross, he says the rest is easy.

Easy for a man who has a PhD in chemistry. For the rest of us, it's still complicated. But the point that I can understand is that there must be a starting place in the jumbled cube. The starting place is the cross. Doesn't that sound like our world? We're a complicated jumble of contrasting pieces, each color desiring to dominate but never having enough to fill out the pattern. But place the cross into the center and the order begins to form. The cross is the center of our puzzle and the answer within our cube.

HYMNS OF FORGIVENESS

While so many more hymns could be cited, two remain as we close with our focus on the cross. Forgiveness flows from the cross and all that Jesus has done. "Go, My Children, with My Blessing" reminds us beautifully of the forgiveness that comes from hearing His story:

> Go, My children, sins forgiven,
>   At peace and pure.
> Here you learned how much I love you,
>   What I can cure.
> Here you heard My dear Son's story;
>   Here you touched Him, saw His glory.
> Go, My children, sins forgiven,
>   At peace and pure. (*LSB* 922:2)

In the end, forgiveness flows from the cross. Let the cross be at the center of your thoughts as you sing one final stanza. Perhaps no hymn says it better than "Abide with Me":

> Hold Thou Thy cross before my closing
>   eyes;
> Shine through the gloom, and point me to
>   the skies.
> Heav'n's morning breaks, and earth's vain
>   shadows flee;
> In life, in death, O Lord, abide with me.
>   (*LSB* 878:6)

Our certainty is that God does abide with us, forgiving us freely for the sake of His Son on the cross. Forgiveness has many facets and expressions but only one center. We meet God, His work, and His forgiveness at the cross.

DISCUSSION QUESTIONS

1. All this time that we've been talking about the cube, did you see the cube being turned into a cross? We've used the cube and the cross as our images of forgiveness, but perhaps you have another shape that speaks of forgiveness. What might that be?

2. The Clean panel in the center of my cross is likely the most important place. If you agree, why are Clean and the color white the natural center for our cross? But if you disagree, which of our six panels and colors/woods would you have at the center?

3. We normally don't put the most expensive pieces out of sight. You wouldn't use walnut for the hidden back of a drawer. However, how is that a good picture of the sacrifice of Christ, completed in the darkness of the cross?

4. The extended horizontal arm is the color blue and the wood is butternut. The idea of Far suggests we make that arm a bit longer. How else might we picture the idea that God has taken our sins far away from us?

5. The color green is for the part of the cross just coming out of the ground. Let green grass be tall around this part of the cross. How is this a good match to the beginning of our biblical story in the Garden of Eden, and how is it also an answer to the curse of thorns and thistles coming because of our sins (Genesis 3)?

6. The uppermost panel is red with the idea of One. One quiet answer from the Father is the last word we hear. One oak tree could supply all we need to stand on. How is this ending of a single word from the Father enough for our questions?

7. Given our six ideas of Clean and Covered, Fixed and Far, Many and One, how would you have arranged them on the six panels of a cross? What other symbols would you have used to convey these six ideas?